DAMAGED GOODS

AN HONEST, HUMOROUS COLLECTION OF SHORT ESSAYS
REVOLVING AROUND MY EXPERIENCE LOSING MY FATHER TO
PROSTATE CANCER, AND ITS LASTING EFFECTS LONG AFTER
THE FUNERAL.

JOHN COLBERT

COLBERT STUDIOS

To Pookie,

Thank you for making me. Just don't die for a while. This book was exhausting, and I'm not ready to write another one.

Love,
Your favorite son

FOREWORD

The following essays are composed of my favorite experiences with my father, as well as some of the most comical ones I experienced once he was gone. There was no manual handed to me on how to grieve or what to expect when your dad dies. His death continues to affect my life in different ways, and I imagine it will until I pass away. Finding the humor in my grief continues to be my survival trait. Hopefully this isn't the worst book you read this year.

Contents

STAGE 4: HERE THE FUCK WE GO

STAGE 5: FINDING COMFORT IN ALL THE WEIRD PLACES

STAGE 6: EMERGING VICTORIOUS AND DELIRIOUS

PREFACE
WELCOME TO THE CRYING CLUB

You might think you're an emotionally stable person or not much of a 'crier,' but wait until you lose a loved one. It's like breaking an arm that heals to about 72 percent of what it once was. On the surface it looks brand-spanking-new, but on the inside it's so sensitive and fragile that if so much as a kitten bumps into it, your brain tells you to get into the fetal position and scream, "MY ARM IS BROKEN!" Hopefully if you do this long enough, someone will swoop in offering free hugs and edibles, but usually when grief strikes, you're in the pasta aisle at Whole Foods, and the only concerned voice you hear is a Prime shopper who needs you to roll to the side so they can get to the vegan parmesan cheese.

The truth is there are no rules when it comes to grieving. Grief doesn't follow any, nor should you. It does whatever it wants whenever it wants, such as making you uber-sensitive and somewhat of a loon bag, causing those around you to slowly back away and delete your name from their contacts. Yes, it will eventually give you a unique superpower that we'll get to later, but at first it offers zero benefits. Instead of being able to lift cars and jump off buildings, you cry... uncontrollably. It's as great as it sounds.

The first time I learned this was months after my dad's funeral, after I had returned to college. I was at Gold's Gym in Keene, New Hampshire, about to crush 'cardio' day. This should've involved things like burpees and interval training to boost heart rate and metabolism, but this was the early 2000s, so 'cardio' back then meant running half-assed on the treadmill for not even a mile or gliding on the elliptical like an empty nester for a half hour.

I chose the treadmill.

I also chose a sweet mix on my MP3 player, though unfortunately I didn't realize I had put a song on that mix three years prior, when my dad was doing pretty well and life was grand: "The Kiss" by Trevor Jones. Unless you're Trevor Jones or a huge *The Last of the Mohicans* fan, that song probably means nothing to you. For me, ever since 2003, that song and the overall soundtrack are a huge emotional trigger. Doesn't matter where I am; if I hear *The Last of the Mohicans* soundtrack—which is usually only via my headphones because no one randomly plays that but me—my heart convulses and the tears just start rolling down my cheeks at a rapid rate. It's a whole thing.

Why? That movie, along with the book it was based on, was one of my dad's favorites. He brought me to see it in the theater, and he loved the movie so much he bought the soundtrack and would blast it from his car. It would emit from the seven-speaker Bose sound system with such rich, lifelike musicality that if we didn't know any better, we would've assumed we were both running through a meadow to save a beauty like Madeleine Stowe from "the bad" Native Americans.

Hearing that song for the first time since his death was like suddenly finding the on switch for tears and just letting that baby rip. Before I knew it, I was doing that thing that irrational, unstable people do—crying in public. From atop an old, creaky treadmill at a Gold's in small-town New Hampshire no less. Classy, party of one right here. The tears started to build, and in a confused, panic state I looked around like, *Wh—what is happening to me? I don't cry... ever??*

Like a stranger in a foreign land, I wanted someone to explain to me in clear English what I was experiencing, and more importantly how to make it go away, but even the rapey-looking guy watching women on the adductor/abductor machine took his eyes off a coed to give me a disappointed look. Feeling embarrassed and stressed, I did the most sensible thing I could think of. I pretended the treadmill was broken, did a few fake "ughs!" while hitting it like a caveman, and then walked away sniffling.

This, my friends, is part of the grieving process... and it never goes away. Once you lose a loved one, you are forever transformed. You will now do things or feel things you hadn't before. Your mind becomes an emotional roller coaster that no one wants to voluntarily ride. To grieve is to fall apart. To scream when you'd normally be calm. To kick and thrash like you're thirteen and pissed that Mom won't let you eat ice cream for dinner. When you lose a loved one, and in my case my father, you join a special club. It's like the Masters Tournament, when the winner is awarded a green blazer, but in the Fallen Fathers Club, instead of being good at golf, you're just really good at crying. When I joined the club, it was pretty lonely, but now, in my forties, I'm seeing more and more of my friends becoming members. Is the club fun? Nah. Does it get you discounted movie passes or frozen yogurt? Nope. But as a friend said recently after losing his father, "The club gets bigger with time, so it could be really cool one day."

Amen, brother.

The crying in public *will get* better over the years, but not when it's a special occasion like a wedding. Especially not when it's your own and you can request who makes the speeches. My father, for instance, was mentioned in every other sentence for an entire long weekend in Long Beach, California, in April 2017. I cried during our vows; I cried during other people's toasts. Heck, I even cried after everyone flew back to the East Coast. It was partially my fault. I asked good people like my brother-in-law Todd to make a speech honoring the one man who couldn't make it that day. Most of the room was teary, though some of my West Coast friends that I hadn't known for too long were probably like, "Man, this wedding is weird as hell!"

My cousin Chris, who is my dad's niece, came up to me after the ceremony. "Why did you want to talk about him so much if it makes you sad?"

"Because he would've loved to be here. I like paying tribute to him."

That seemed to be a justified response because she gave me a heartfelt smile, a consoling pat on the shoulder, then pelvis-thrusted her way back onto the dance floor as the opening riff to "Return of the Mack" played.

If you haven't lost a parent yet, when you do, you'll quickly see how obsessed you'll become with maintaining their legacy. You'll find it's worth the tears. When you're around family, you'll want to bring them up often. "Remember how Dad used to do the white man's overbite at parties?" Or, "This pasta is great. Remember Dad's red sauce recipe?" Your memories and even their personal possessions suddenly skyrocket in value. A dumb General Electric alarm clock they had on their bedside table is now 'priceless.' If you have siblings and your parents are still alive, start slapping Post-its on that shit ASAP. If you don't have siblings, then I feel bad for you because your holidays are probably boring, but I envy you because you'll get it all when they're gone. Including the unwanted tears.

There truly is no manual for this stuff. How to cope with life once a loved one starts dying *and* how to cope with life once they're gone are two stages I fumbled through like a drunk giraffe. There weren't any good guidelines, rules, or tips. Well, there probably were/are, but I'm not into self-help books. I find most to be long-winded and cheesy. My first therapist (that should tell you something) gave me a book on death and dying. I read a chapter or two, used it to prop open a door for a while, and then fifteen years later used it as a reference to write this book.

The point is, when my father was dying, no one else knew what I was going through. Besides my family, all of my friends and classmates were oblivious. Fraternity brothers would drunkenly console me at parties, but I was surrounded by people that hadn't been down this shitty road before. In the US the average life expectancy is seventy-eight. My dad passed away at fifty-six! Many kids unfortunately experience divorce, but hey, at least both parents are still living. Trust me, I'd trade!

Back when it happened, I thought my situation was more normal. I thought everyone would lose a parent around age sixty. I've learned over the years, though, that a parent having cancer is rare, and what's even more rare is them passing away from it. My mom, whom my sisters and I call Pookie, is a two-time breast cancer survivor while most moms at her age only know the trauma that comes from peeing when they sneeze. Amateurs. I've also learned that most men who get diagnosed with prostate cancer are able to treat it and survive. I especially love hearing this every time I get my annual physical.

"You know, now most men are able to detect it early and treat it," my doctor said to me a few months ago.

"You know no men in my situation want to hear stuff like this, right?" I replied.

From the moment my father went into the intensive care unit to the present day, I've had twenty years of bizarre, grief-related encounters, experiences, and observations that are too good not to share. This is because they are legitimately good or because I was raised to overshare, regardless of a story's quality. Growing up in the Colbert household, you quickly learned that sharing a humorous, self-deprecating experience was the only way to get attention at the dinner table. You sharted during recess? Gather everyone around and tell them about it. The loudest one wins, but the funniest one gets out of doing the dishes.

While writing this book was cathartic for me, hopefully it can also offer a form of comfort to those that might be freshly grieving. A little validation or amusement, if you will, or at least a slight distraction to those who are reading on a packed public bus that smells like feet. As my mother, Pookie, would say, "the reality is" grieving is the worst, and while it's abnormal to most, it's normal to me. That's why I compiled the following collection of humorous stories into the brand-spankin'-new John Colbert Six Stages of Grief (patent pending). It's about what life was like when my father's cancer got bad, what life was like after he passed, and it even has some entertaining memories that stand out when I reflect on him as a father. He was a smart, charming, ambitious, and witty man who was always trying to teach me things, like the fine art of sarcasm and networking. Jack Colbert continues to teach me things to this day. I imagine he will until the day I die. For the record, this book will teach you literally nothing.

With that, I say enjoy!

Sincerely,
　　John

THE COLBERTS
august 2000

Jack "Pake"

Sarah

Cheryl "Pookie"

brother in law Todd

Sami

Natalie

JOHN COLBERT'S SIX STAGES OF GRIEF

STAGE 1: DENIAL TOWN, USA

Everything is wonderful, haven't you heard?

CHAPTER 1
WHAT THE FRAPPE

THERE WAS a point during my dad's last few months where things seemed to be getting shockingly better. You see, for six years his bout with cancer was a battle he was actually winning. Until he went into the ER on New Year's Eve, 2001, it never felt totally life-and-death. Just days after he started his first round of chemo, it felt like the latter—like his days were drastically numbered—but after the holidays, his stats miraculously improved and everyone's morale started to climb. His doctors now had the confidence to allow him to check out of the ICU at Brigham & Women's and check into the Spaulding Rehab facility. This was progress. It meant he was ready to dive into his next step of recovery from the chemo treatments, which I've nicknamed, as of the writing of this book, "Operation: Walk the Line." You see, because he had so many cancerous tumors—specifically one on his spine—his legs were useless. He had to learn how to walk again.

I know what you're thinking: *This... sounds... DEPRESSING.* Well, yeah, but compared to where he had been, this was heaven. It's like an upgrade to extra leg room when you've been flying in coach for eight hours. February was our Main Cabin Extra. Dad got to stay in other places besides the intense, depressing ICU. Like home. He spent a few nights at his own house, and he even had the pleasure of watching his sisters who had flown in from Florida change his linens. I don't believe in God, but someone granted all us Colberts with an incredible, dark sense of humor. It's probably the best survival trait you can have during times like these.

Though Dad was home, it was only a matter of time, usually days, before one of his monitors would beep like a lunatic and he would be forced to go back into one of the various hospitals his doctors had approved. But the variety of locations, no matter how short-lived any of them were, made everyone, including my father, happy. I especially liked Spaulding because they were legit when it came to muscular, neurological, and sports injury rehab. They had a great staff, and there were far fewer visitors crying in the hallways than I was used to. We were happy to have their help.

And, until a request he made one day, my father was happy to have mine.

"I want a Brigham's shake," he said.

"A frappe?" I replied.

He nodded with a smile. He asked no one else. Just me. This was my assignment. Between the two of us, I was the only one that could carry it out. I could walk and I could drive.

Established in 1914, Brigham's Ice Cream is a New England staple. Up until the nineties, they were set up as ice cream parlors, the kind where you could get an ice cream sundae in an old-fashioned silver dish. Beyond the sundaes their pièce de résistance was their frappes. "A milkshake" to an outsider, but to a Brigham's die-hard fan, they're frappes. Frappes are thick as fuck and tasty as hell. Sure, Häagen Dazs and Ben & Jerry's are great, but Brigham's is nostalgic. My father, having grown up in Dorchester, was a big fan. We would get frappes often after soccer games on Saturdays or after dinner on a humid summer night. My best friend, Greg, and I would try to get whichever parent was doing carpool to stop at the one in Newton after we got picked up from soccer practice at prep school.

"Wait, can we get Brigham's?!" one of us gangly, tween males in the back of the Dodge minivan would yell, our voices cracking, braces tearing the inside of our mouths in the process. It was hit-or-miss. You never knew how the driver of the day was going to respond. Sometimes the parent who was driving would roll their eyes or instantly shout, "No!," but if you asked for Brigham's in the presence of Jack Colbert, it was a sure thing. He did his part for years in making sure that my skinny-ass frame got a thousand calories in one sitting. Now it was my time to return the favor.

"Okay, so one mint chocolate chip frappe with vanilla ice cream?" I confirmed as I put my coat on. My dad, lying in his hospital bed, reading something intelligent, turned to me and calmly said, "Yes, thank you, John."

I left and did something dumb. I let someone help me with my mission.

"What does your dad want?" Pookie asked as she entered the kitchen.

I had stopped at home since it was en route to Brigham's to

3

grab a quick snack. Rookie move. Pookie was now slowly infiltrating the mission.

"He wants a mint chocolate chip frappe from Brigham's."

Her face pursed up. That's when I knew I was in the danger zone. Like I'd stepped unsuspecting into quicksand—I was slowly being sucked into her controlling method of helping— which didn't always produce great results.

"Brigham's is far. We can just make him a shake here."

That's when I should've closed the fridge, grabbed my keys, and never looked back. The fact that she was calling it a "shake" was the first red flag. But hindsight is 20/20. The events that would occur in that kitchen birthed an amount of shame that will always be in my soul. The only defense I put up was skepticism as I asked, "With what ingredients?"

Then I watched the Pookster as she shimmied along the kitchen floor in her Lands' End corduroy pants and socks, creating what can only be imagined as the largest amount of static electricity ever produced. She moved with such gusto, determination, and awful standards. A jar of wheat germ from one cabinet, the expiration date questionably faded. A carton of skim milk; not even the good, fatty whole milk. She was grabbing the most random, disgusting ingredients.

"Mom, let me just go," I protested. "It'll be easy."

"Nonsense. Ooh, we *do* have protein powder!"

She was excited. I was not. The protein powder she was grabbing was made by Nikken, a brand that no one had heard about except for my uncle Fred. He's obsessed with it. They make mostly magnetic products. Yup, magnets. The idea according to him—because, yes, he's a sales rep for Nikken—is that there is an electronic current running through the human body. It escapes through our extremities, but magnets help contain it. And when it's harnessed, it can help with strength, balance, and even alleviate stress and illness. Truthfully I wore the insoles for years. I was already wearing orthotics, so pack it on, I figured. I don't remember seeing incredible results, but my lower back didn't hurt back then, so maybe I should get some magnets back in my life. Anyway, Nikken had a whole slew of wellness products, including protein powder that tasted like an old attic.

"One scoop is good," Pookie said to herself as she plopped the powder into the old Black and Decker.

"I almost forgot!" she said with a sudden, happy urgency. This woman was loving a task that no one, especially my dad, had asked her to do. She reached into the freezer and took out a carton of Breyers. As she peeled back the lid, the freezer burn was so intense it was screaming. I made a face like I had just smelled a fart. God help us. Using a big spoon, because our ice cream scooper committed suicide years ago, she struggled to scoop out the ice cream. Maybe because it was mostly ice! The spoon bent a little, but she got it. The woman was a survivor, y'all.

WURRRRR! The blender sped as her finger held the button down like a sociopath. What can I say? The woman had mysterious skills. She could get appliances to work that had shit the bed years ago, yet she couldn't close up a bag of chips properly to save her life. After minutes of blending, she poured the contents into a travel coffee mug. It looked brown even though she had used a vanilla chocolate chip ice cream. Maybe it was the wheat germ that turned it into a sad beige? Or she might've thrown in wood chips when I wasn't looking. So much was tossed in the blender for this "shake" that anything is possible. Wait a minute, where's our cat Muffin?

Ten minutes later I was back at Spaulding, pulling into a parking space.[1] I was in my dad's 1997 forest-green Jeep Wrangler. He had bought it used as a "Nantucket car." That's how New England White™ we are. That's also how much fun he could be. Always nervous I'd grow up spoiled, he never gave me the car, just let me "borrow it" at times. This was a parenting move I now greatly respect. The guilt wasn't lost on me as I pulled into that parking lot in a fun car he had paid for, toting a sad shake that I didn't pay for, thus sacrificing quality and, more importantly, nostalgia for a man that was living life like a WWII vet these days.

Did the look of disappointment appear on my father's face once he saw the travel mug? Or was it already there because he knew if I had gone to Brigham's I wouldn't have been back so soon? To be honest I can't recall. But I do remember the look on his face when he took a sip. It was not anger; it was more like sadness.

"How is it?" I asked.

He shook his head, unable to speak around the icy turd that was now in his mouth. I laughed and tried to defend myself. Yes, I mentioned how I tried to talk Pookie out of it. Yes, I did say it had good protein powder in it. (*Magnetic* protein powder, I might add!) But my father was never one to be won over by

---

1. Why I didn't just dump out the DIY shake and head to Brigham's is a thought that never crossed my mind. But logic was an endangered species during times like these.

excuses, no matter how valid they might have been. He was a results man, and that day I produced C- results.

"Here, just put it over there for now," he said with a slight smile. He was trying to compensate for his lukewarm reaction, but we both knew the truth. My dad never asked for another favor after that. Maybe because he passed away two months later. Or maybe it was because he no longer could trust me. Maybe that sad excuse for a milkshake made him lose all hope. Then again, the next day he said, "Watch this!" and was able to walk holding the balance beams in the gym for all of ten seconds. Spaulding Rehab knew what they were doing. But maybe, just maybe, The Pookie Shake was the athlete fuel he needed. Forget Ensure or Gatorade. What old and/or ailing people need is a scientific formula of freezer-burned ice cream and expired wheat germ.

Unfortunately, this tale only gets worse. The Brigham's Ice Cream in Wellesley, Mass., was laid to rest a year or so later. That was the location I would've gone to to get my dad his Make-A-Wish request for a mint chocolate chip frappe. You can still buy their ice cream in grocery stores, but the physical locations no longer exist.

I like to imagine, because I'm a masochist, a reporter tracking down whoever the last manager of that Wellesley Brigham's was. It takes months for this plucky reporter to find them, and, in a cliché but awesome way, this curmudgeonly person now lives in an old house on a small, sad pond in the Catskills, two hundred miles from any ice cream shop. Here this retired manager has full-blown conversations with a feral cat they call "Steve." When this reporter comes to their house, no one answers the door, so they have to run around back to find the person just staring out at the water like a troubled soul. When questioned about what really happened when they closed up shop back in 2002, the old, dead-inside ice cream parlor manager will take their eyes off the scenery for the first time in ten minutes, turn to the reporter, and just mutter the words, "Three ninety-five."

Our very likeable protagonist will ask, confused, "What's three ninety-five?"

"We were in the red by three dollars and ninety-five cents. Corporate had a zero-red policy." Then he or she will turn back to the lake and take a sip of their cheap beer and be furious for the rest of the day that they were reminded of a traumatic incident they have spent so many years learning how to forget.

Moments later the reporter will head back to their car. They'll get in revealing that their lover, most likely a co-worker, is riding shotgun, dying to know how it went. "Well?" they'll ask.

The reporter, strained in thought as they stare at the keyless ignition switch, will pause. Without taking their eyes off it, they'll ask, "How much was a milkshake—I mean, a frappe—back in the early 2000s?"

The friend will say, "Three ninety-five, why?"

The reporter will smirk. The lover will ask, "Everything all right?," and the reporter will turn and look at them lovingly and let out a vague "yeah." The lover won't ask questions because that's how it works on TV.

The screen fades to black. The producers win nine Emmys.

The irony of it all is that Pookie now has six cartons of Brigham's in her fridge on any given day. Last time I was home,

I opened the freezer and jumped back a foot. "Good god, Mom!"

She slowly, and I mean *slowly,* walked over to see what the commotion was.

"Anything wrong with this picture?" I asked.

She looked at all the cartons of ice cream on the shelves.

"Here, I'll start," I said. "I count six." I looked around the house, then back to her. "I count one of you."

"Anytime they go on sale I buy some!" she said defensively.

"How are none of these freezer-burned? That's so unlike you!"

By the time I turned back she was giving me a death glare. "Do you want some or not? I'm gonna have a bowl," she said as she plucked the carton of Brigham's Strawberry out of the freezer.

"Mom, it's three p.m."

"So?"

I sighed. "Remember frappes?" I muttered. "Those were great."

She turned around quickly. "The blender is around here somewhere. We could make one."

No, Pookie. Apparently, we can't.

CHAPTER 2
BAD TIMING, GOOD PATTY MELTS

TWO WEEKS before my twenty-first birthday, my father did something super frustrating.

He died.

Granted it was from prostate cancer, so his excuse was quite valid. But couldn't he have at least waited until I was fifty-five and more financially and emotionally secure? Instead he left me when I was 135 pounds of insecure stupidity. I was like a bowling ball that constantly needed the inflatable bumpers to keep it from going in the gutter as it heads toward the pins. Losing my dad was like losing one of those. Did I just do a bowling analogy? Yes, I did. My dad is dead, and I can do whatever I want.

It didn't help that his timing was less than ideal in multiple ways. For years my father and I had fought. Then, the moment we became besties, he was like, "All right, world! Jacky out!"

Years prior had been a constant struggle for the two of us. Take when I was in high school for instance. We fought almost every day. He wanted me to move mountains, and I wanted to move cushions to find the ideal level of comfort on the living room couch. The silver lining of our fraught relationship was that it taught me the fine art of sarcasm. While both of us were yelling, I would use it to get out my frustrations, and sometimes he'd crack up. That was my strongest weapon. The annoying part of these arguments, though, was that he was the Managing Director at a prestigious Boston law firm. To say he picked up some impressive debate tricks from his fellow lawyers was an understatement. I'd get all worked up, and he'd be calm and intelligent.

"This isn't a hotel. You can't just come and go," he'd say as we set the table for dinner.

"I WISH IT WAS. THEN I'D HAVE ROOM SERVICE! UGH, I HATE YOUUUUUUU!" I'd scream.

"Why are you yelling?" he'd ask.

"BECAUSE I'M ANGRY!" I'd bark.

"Do you think my lawyers yell when they get mad in court?" he'd state.

"NO, BUT THEY SHOULD!" Then I'd make a fart sound effect and punch the wall as I stormed up to my room. He would stand there waiting as I made a U-turn on the stairs and returned, realizing this argument had taken place as we were setting the table and I still needed to eat. I'd grab a plate, sit down, and proceed to eat while trying to mentally be in the Bahamas.

This routine took place 80 percent of the time until I graduated. Then college happened. Suddenly I wasn't home every night, and I was now nineteen, so my dad felt like he didn't have to manage me anymore. It was like I was someone else's employee. He'd come to visit me at school and be happy to see me, no matter what. I'd open a bedroom door to introduce him to my friends down the hall and a cloud of weed would slap us both in the face.

We'd then walk outside to his car.

"Any longer and I'd be floating home," he'd say and we'd both chuckle.

Guess it was simple. I was out of the nest, and my dad didn't have to worry as much about me. He was also doing well health-wise. He was doing radiation here and there, and his cancer was in remission. In his mind, life was short, so it wasn't worth micromanaging his only son anymore.

It was junior year. I was in college. My dad didn't yell at me as much anymore. We even joked around together sometimes. Life was great. And then that metaphorical asteroid comes barreling towards us.

Of course, I'm speaking of death.

At this point, it had been five years that my dad had been fighting the C-word. My parents were dressed to the nines, driving to their friends' annual New Year's Eve party, when Dad suddenly felt a slight pain in his chest.

"Nope, this isn't good. Are you having a shortness of breath? What are your symptoms?" said my mom, who apparently lives and dies by the unspoken motto of *Once a nurse, always be really annoying about medical stuff.*[1]

"Cher, I'm fine. Let's just get to the party," my dad said. Then he winced in pain and clutched his chest through his starched, ruffled tux shirt.

---

[1] Pookie went to nursing school when she and my father were dating and later became a nurse practitioner.

"No," Mom insisted. "We are getting you to a hospital!"

My mom was always the kind of nurse who had to make sure everyone knew she was a nurse. She also felt like she could heal, fix, and cure anyone and anything. A woman passed out on a flight we were taking once. The flight attendants tended to her while my mom stood up, kneeled on her seat, and turned around so she could face the situation that was unfolding two to three rows behind us. She proceeded to inform everyone around us of what was 'probably' going on and what 'probably' would have to be done to fix it. Complete strangers slowly approached aisle seat 15B so that they could better hear every prognosis coming from Cheryl Colbert's mouth. Meanwhile, my sisters and I slunk down further and further into our seats, feeling like if only we had a Phillips-head screwdriver, then we could remove the panel below our seats and crawl down into steerage. Anything to avoid the embarrassing tractor beam my mother was putting out into economy class.

But thanks to Cheryl's nurse-like instincts, she got my dad to the ER that night. And it's a good thing she did. They found a little surprise the next day when his test results came back.

"About nine tumors total," the doctor casually told us. His cadence alone might have made us believe they were just bug bites. Maybe he had had a patient last week who had thirty-five tumors, so yeah, nine was child's play.

"Nine tumors?!" my mom screamed.

"Yes," he said. "One in the chest, which explains those chest pains. Then a few on the base of the spine, one behind your left eye..." He went on and on. Once they told me about the first couple, I was like, "Okay, yeah. We're fucked." What're tumors five, six, seven, eight, and nine gonna do that one through four can't already destroy on their own?

My father then began what I like to call the Cocktail of Death. He began chemo and what would become his all-inclusive, six-month vacation at the intensive care unit at the Dana-Farber in Boston. Just like at a Sandals resort, he'd be surrounded by unfortunate-looking bodies and the food to match.

That is, the food was gross unless you were a visitor and could wander down to the cafeteria because you had things like freedom and a clean bill of health. This is where my Dad's-dying-of-cancer security blanket, also known as Pat's Place, existed.

Dana-Farber is a very renowned hospital. Some of the most brilliant minds in the country practice medicine there. While their food court circa 2002 wasn't a replica of Grand Central's in Manhattan, the mini diner called Pat's Place had a flat top grill and wasn't afraid to use it. They made what I still consider to this day one of the most fantastic tuna melts I have ever had. My older sister, Sami, and I would visit my dad, try not to burst into tears, and then take the elevator down to Pat's Place to find happiness in an unlikely spot: warm cheddar cheese draped over scoops of tuna, all pressed between two buttery, toasted slices of white bread. I was twenty, so I had the metabolism of a racehorse. Otherwise I would've easily gained two hundred pounds and have been carried to my car via forklift.

Over the course of three months, the chemo aged my father greatly. He went in with a full head of hair and a sweet set of

'BT's' (or bitch tits) and transformed into what I can only describe as one of the old guys you see Smuckers give a shout-out to on *The Today Show*: *Bill is from Woonsocket, Rhode Island. He's 105, and he says his secret to longevity is his stamp collection!*

This transformation happened in light-years. I learned just how fast when I came back after only being at school for three or four weeks and thought I had the wrong room. The man in front of me was a corpse. A frail, old man with a few gray pubes for hair. Where was the fifty-six-year-old guy I sometimes called "Dad" and most of the time "Ugh, hi, Dad"? Where was the guy that played golf more often than Pookie would have liked and could crush the 'white man's overbite' on the dance floor? Apparently that man, a.k.a. Dad, was right there in front of me. But I didn't believe it, so I left and never came back.

Kidding! Of course I stayed. I stayed for a whole five minutes because that's when my nose thought it smelled grilled cheese, which then made my stomach go, "Tuna melt time??"

My point is, I didn't recognize him. Cancer is cruel in that and so many other ways. He looked like my grandfather, who was twenty-five years older than he was. My dad's hair was still whitish-gray, but it seemed like he had less of it now. I even washed it one day. He stayed in bed while I gave him an epic shampoo, then the messiest rinse of all time. We both laughed in the process. Sure, the nurses were changing his linens, his catheter, serving him three meals a day and watching him throughout all hours of the night, but were they giving him that Vidal Sassoon treatment?! I didn't think so!

Other times I helped didn't go as smoothly. Like the time I helped him go from the hospital bed to the chair so he could 'change it up.' Me being a gym rat and a tool, I was like, "Yup, I can lift him." I stood behind him and lifted him from under his arms. He was surprisingly heavy, but you forget when someone isn't moving to help you, it's like dead weight. He hung limply while I grunted and laughed and got him in the chair. He smiled and thanked me. Then we moved on. But when I came back the next day and the nurse was changing his shirt, I suddenly lost my breath. All under his armpits and arms where I had lifted him, he was covered in bruises. I felt horrible.

The hospital visits were a sobering experience, not really how my fellow classmates at Keene State were spending their weekends. For that reason, even though I was still going to classes and living with my roommates off campus, I started distancing myself from the college world a bit. I was physically there but not mentally. I felt like an old man myself, surrounded by kids. My frat brothers, for instance, would complain about someone throwing up during a party in the first-floor bathroom's shower, and they weren't joking. They were furious and annoyed that this was happening weekly, like they couldn't imagine how it could happen with all those kegs and plastic liters of Aristocrat Vodka. I found myself starting to skip those Sunday night meetings, along with the parties. It all seemed so trivial compared to what my family was dealing with. The college world would be my comforting savior down the road, but for the time being, I was subconsciously starting to mourn.

My dad was always happy when I came to visit. Maybe because I was his only son. The heir to his throne. The great male descendant who had inherited his signature flat feet! More likely it was because I could only come every few weeks, so when I came around, it was 'refreshing.' My visits were nice but nothing spectacular. I'd usually swing by the old West Coast Video where I had worked throughout high school and get hooked up with the latest action movie. Then I'd bring it to my dad's hospital room so we could watch together. He would fall asleep ten minutes in or say he was kind of exhausted and just wanted to rest and read the paper. (This kinda felt like bullshit since I had driven forty minutes to visit him, and had I known he was just gonna pass out I would've watched *Face/Off* at home and saved on gas money. Oh well. Don't have to deal with that ever again!)

My older sisters didn't get as warm of a welcome, which naturally I enjoyed hearing. They would often use their lunch breaks to drop by and give him unconditional love, emotional support, and, more importantly, the *Boston Globe*, and most of the time he would just say, "You guys should really be at work," and politely get them to leave. They started taking time off because it was too hard to focus, but my dad would get mad at them for missing work, so they started putting on work clothes even on their days off. That way, he would think they were going back to work after they visited. They visited often because they are caring souls, and they lived in the area. I think that's why all of this was harder on them and my mom than it technically was on me at the time. Don't get me wrong, I was falling apart at the seams, but I could escape to college and distract myself if I wanted to with drama at the frat house, my sweet saltwater fish tank, and oh yeah, my ex-girlfriend.[2]

While I tried to enjoy being a junior in college, my father

---

2. To Sydney's credit she was a nice girlfriend and very supportive. I just know

went in and out of the ICU. We'd all get excited because he'd be greenlit to go home, but then a week later his condition would get worse and he'd need all the badass machines at Dana-Farber to keep him stable.

Then one morning my sister Sami called me crying hysterically. "John, it's Sami. Dad isn't doing well. You gotta get down here as soon as you can!"

I slowly hung up the phone, and a smooth wave of anxiety crashed over me.

My dad was on the waiting list for heaven.

And I was two hours away.

To say I drove recklessly was an understatement. To say my car at the time was a way-too-much-fun, forest-green Jeep Wrangler was quite accurate. I grabbed a duffel, tossed whatever I could find into it, and peeled out of the driveway. One of my roommates probably exited his room in his boxers, half asleep, wondering, *Does this mean Colbert isn't coming to twenty-five-cent wing night?*

When I arrived, speeding ticket free, everyone from my dad's side of the family was there, all huddled in a 'family waiting area' and all taking turns crying. I could tell this from their eyes, the balled-up tissues in their hands, and because the room reeked of malaise.

"John! You made it!" said my aunt Judy, who is a phenomenal hugger, I might add. She proved her skills and then stepped away. I looked around the room and then down to the floor out of shyness. For the first time in fifteen years, I broke

---

my wife will smile greatly if I take an ex down a peg every time one is mentioned.

down crying in front of everyone. The dam had opened, and it felt glorious to let it flow. I was blubbering hard. I was embarrassed but also couldn't help it. It's like I had delayed being emotional for an hour and forty-five minutes on my drive from New Hampshire, so when I entered that waiting room, my heart was like, "NOW LET'S DO THIS." Everyone suddenly rushed to hug me. It was nice.

Ten minutes later I was sitting in a quiet conference room with just my mother and two older sisters. Our youngest sister, Natalie, stayed behind since she was too young. This was like one of those scenes in an action movie when everyone important at the Pentagon gathers around a fancy table to discuss the terrorist threat level and how a Harrison Ford or Steven Seagal type will take action against them. Except we weren't in some cool room with lit-up computers in the background and men in decorated uniforms briefing us. Instead, we were in a sterile hospital conference room with one piece of shitty art on the wall and the faint smell of a lack of showering on all of us across the board.

Our father's primary physician entered the room and closed the door behind him. He quickly got to the point. My father's condition had gotten drastically worse, so much so that he would not be able to function without some sort of breathing/feeding tube going down his throat twenty-four seven. An endotracheal tube, to be exact. The doctor explained, calmly I might add, that they'd monitor my dad for a few days to see if his system improved and if he could be weaned off the feeding tube. In three days we would reconvene with the doctor and see the results. If he couldn't become independent of the tube, then we had to make a bigger call as a family: introduce my father at parties as Jack Colbert, the Vegetable, or, equally as bad, Jack Colbert, the Deceased.

Sami and Sarah took turns crying. Pookie couldn't ask enough questions. She even became combative with the physician. He was treating this a little too casually in her opinion.

I didn't know who to support, so I just sat there, going into autopilot mode. When times get tough, I fire off depth charges in the form of jokes that offer no value to the present situation. "Maybe we can throw him a bone by extending the tube down to Pat's Place," I said. I then nudged Sami for a laugh, but she didn't flinch. She had become numb to the world. Which makes sense. I was just an emotionally immature sociopath or I would've responded the same way. Either that or the joke was so bad she didn't want to acknowledge it.

We all nodded in agreement with the doc's plan, knowing the odds were not in our favor. What else were we supposed to do? This was also our first rodeo. Well, technically, we had been to a legit rodeo in Wyoming, but as far as someone dying, this was our first jaunt. In keeping with the rodeo metaphor, we knew we were gonna get mauled by a bull in three days, but all we could do was focus on the present. Keep Dad in the fight. Three days. That was the new timeline to wait and see if the man could be saved or not. If you're thinking to yourself, *Wow, the Colberts are some impatient bastards!*, you'd be right! But in this case, according to the pros, that was plenty of time to test whether Dad could bounce back or forever need to be on life support.

At this point, while it sounds heartless, I was ready for him to go. The last six months had been so heavy and awful for him that I just wanted him to be happy. I knew for someone as successful and smart as him, reading the *Globe* a day or two behind everyone else was not 'happiness.' Nor was watching other people play golf via ESPN. Selfishly I was drained too. I didn't know how much longer I could stay in this 'my dad is dying' mental state.

The three days became a blur. Pookie, Natalie, and I camped out at the house while the phone rang off the hook with calls from my mom's friends. Before we knew it, we were back at Dana-Farber. Back in that conference room that looked like it belonged in a nineties bank. My father's physician took a brief pause before sharing his update, but we didn't need it. We could already tell it wouldn't be good. If he had seemed a little too unfazed days before, he was now definitely fazed. I could see the weight of what had been happening was wearing him down too. By the way, if a doctor ever begins to speak to you very calmly and a notch or two quieter than usual, get your tissues ready. It's never good news. I think their strategy is that if they are soft-spoken you'll subconsciously copy their tone. Clearly they didn't study 'people like the Colberts' in med school. My father's condition had not improved. He was relying heavily on the feeding tube with not an ounce of hope that he would ever not need it. We all became visibly upset.

"Great, glad that the feeding tube worked out," I said to myself, obnoxiously loudly.

One of my sisters shot me a look. Which was valid. The doctor left so we could decide what to do.

We now had to make a choice: pull the plug and say goodbye or keep him going for another week and see if by some miracle he bounced back. Before this moment, I had thought 'pull the plug' was just a dumb phrase characters said in made-for-TV movies. Now I was contemplating doing it for realsies. We debated, but I think all our minds were made up the moment the doctor said Dad wasn't doing any better. While most families in the Boston area were chugging crullers and wicked hot coffee from Dunkin, we marched toward my father's hospital room with the taste of old hospital coffee in our mouths and dried tears on our faces. I took a seat in the corner of his room while Pookie and Sarah flanked my dad's bed.

I shifted in my chair. I didn't know how to sit for something like this. Slouch like who cares? Or sit up straight to pay respect? Ugh, this was stressful. That's when I noticed Pookie's head and eyes darting around the room in quick, rapid motions like a momma bird that lost its baby.

"Where's Sam?" she asked.

"She doesn't want to watch," I said, pointing out Sami, who was now pacing the hallway outside our father's room. Sarah left the room then, and I soon followed. Sami spotted us and rushed over.

"I'm not going in there!" she proclaimed, jacked up on frustration and possibly a Snickers bar she wolfed down when we weren't looking. "This is fucked up, you guys!" She was wearing a disbelieving smirk, as though she could see how absurd all this was.

"You're not gonna wanna miss this," I said.

Sarah chimed in. "We need to say goodbye to him. You don't wanna regret not being able to do that."

Sami was adamant. "It's an image I'll never be able to get out of my head."

She was right. But she hadn't factored in FOMO, so I did.

"Sarah and I are going to recap about this for years, and you won't know what we're talking about 'cause you weren't there!"

We all laughed, an odd response given the circumstances, but with Colbert's humor is a strong coping mechanism.

"Trust me!" Sami said. "You guys can have this moment together. It'll be *your thing*!"

"We'll probably have so many inside jokes from this it'll be great," Sarah said directly to me.

"Maybe it won't be that bad!" I said.

"Oh, really? How many people have you seen die before your eyes?!" Sami yelled.

"Dad will be my first. It'll be great!" I said.

Nurses and personnel were beginning to stare. We didn't care, but we suddenly got quiet on our own. Then in unison we craned our heads to look into Dad's room. I watched as Pookie straightened out a set of 'healing stones' she had attached to a hideous fleece blanket populated by animated M&M characters against a blue background that she had brought from home for my father to use during his stay. I turned back to my sisters. We each took turns taking the biggest eye rolls of our lives. Just then the nurse came up to us.

"Okay, I'm going to remove the feeding tube," she said, "and then you all can enter and be with him. But I ask that you do not enter until I've said so because I want to make sure I've properly removed the tube and that he is safe and happy. I'm going to give him a sedative so he's comfortable when I remove the tube as you say goodbye." Meaning we'd have possibly five minutes to say whatever we wanted to say and be with him until he took his last breath.

Pookie was suddenly by my side. I nearly jumped. I never

saw her exit the room and every year she shrinks five inches, so when suddenly this tiny woman was next to me like a rabid squirrel, of course I reacted in surprise.

A former nurse, as she tells everyone on Earth, she had to chime in.

"Did you say morphine for the pain? I couldn't hear you, sorry."

The nurse nodded. "Yes, morphine will be the sedative to help him be comfortable."

"Morphine, great," Pookie said. She turned and noticed me giving her a look. "What?"

"Why did you repeat that?"

"John, not now," Pookie barked.

I smiled, trying not to laugh and trying to not engage with her. I wanted to play it cool in front of the staff. You know, in case any of them had forgotten the loud and emotionally inappropriate debate my sisters and I had had in the hallway like a pack of hyenas all of five minutes ago.

"I'll go in now. Please do not come in until I've opened the door and said you may do so," the nurse said. She gave us each, one by one, such intense eye contact, so I did what any grown man does and looked down and to the side until she went away.

As I looked down, scared, I watched her rubber-soled shoes quietly scurry past my sight line and toward my father's private room. I looked up to spot Sami biting a nail and reading some dumb plaque on the wall. I decided to do the same. 'Best Patient Care 2001.' Should've said 'Best Tuna Melt.' Maybe the cafeteria had its own wall of awards. I turned around to see how Sarah was enjoying these moments and noticed her biting a nail, too, while trying not to stare at the other nurses at the charge station. Our family plaque would say 'Big on Nail Biting Since 1986.'

Sarah was at least being discreet. She stared like a creep at the nurses' station, but at least she looked away at the first sign of being caught. Pookie took a different approach. There she stood, feet planted smack in front of the glass window that looked into my father's room, waiting for the nurse to pull back the privacy curtain so she could make sure she had extracted the feeding tube correctly. Like it really matters now? Regardless, she didn't bother to look away or bite a nail. She just stood there supervising with skepticism washed all over her face. Pookie was never an ICU nurse, but that doesn't mean she didn't have notes!

Moments later, on the nurse's cue, we shuffled in and took seats around my father's hospital bed. The tube was out, and he was calm, slowly taking breaths, which we knew were soon to be numbered. The nurse closed the door behind her, probably to get a drink or just vent about us in the break room. For her sake, I hope it was a combo of the two.

My father lay in his bed as he always did in the ICU, but he seemed more relaxed now. It was as if he knew it was all over and he could unwind for the first time in six years. He was conscious but not really able to talk. Dad had always been the good host, so it felt like he was really dropping the ball lately. I mean, no music and no drinks? Lame.

The vibe was eerily quiet and a tad awkward. No one knew where or how to begin. Correction, Sarah did.

"Dad... we love you..."

Kiss-ass.

Sami and Pookie followed suit. They were natural. Like

they said "I love you" often. Mine emerged from my mouth with so much nervousness and stage fright that I felt like an ESL student trying to order for the first time at Chili's.

"Dad... I do love... a you?"

A machine beeped. We all looked over and realized his heart rate was getting slower. Man, they really just don't give you a lot of time for these things! He began gasping for air, and little by little, the image went into our memory banks as our brains said to themselves, "Nightmare fuel? Check!"

It was a surreal sight. There my father lay, once a mover and a shaker in the Boston business world. The man had climbed out of an abusive childhood thanks to my awful, alcoholic grandparents and provided such an incredible life for all of us. He was always moving, be it in a suit at a major law firm, a puffy vest and flannel next to a major pile of leaves, or in a polo and shorts with a major 'That's what she said' joke on the tip of his tongue, about to make par on the eighteenth green. But now here he just... lay... like all those Jack Colberts were merely distant memories or different people. My father now looked like Gandalf the Grey, except with way shorter hair and no Screen Actors Guild awards. He lay helpless and tired. He had been at war with his cancer for six years, and the last three months had been by far the hardest. He was done fighting. He was done being the king of his domain. You could tell by the way he was taking periodic gasps of air like a goldfish that had accidently fallen out of the tank but wasn't worried about being saved.

My eyes zoomed out a bit, like a camera getting a wider view, and suddenly I was distracted by what was draped over his chest. The goddamn bright blue fleece blanket Pookie had brought from home– to 'keep him cozy,' as she put it. From my seated position, I was able to get a better view of the healing stones. There were six or seven total, and they looked like Mentos. And by the way, a lot of good those healing stones did. The man was minutes away from heaven. Annoyed, and feeling awkward, I did what only I was comfortable doing. I made fun of it.

"Thank god he has his favorite M&M blanket," I joked. Sami chuckled. Sarah was too teary to laugh, but she'd come around. I was twenty years old. I legitimately didn't know how to talk about feelings yet, but I did know how to make useless jokes.

Sarah tried to keep it heartfelt. "We promise to honor you, Dad, and never forget you," she added. She was good.

Sami chimed in. "I promise to teach Tyler everything about his grandpa Pake."

With that one line about my nephew, my eldest sister had raised the emotional stakes exponentially. I had to even it out again.

"We promise Mike won't be around much longer," I distastefully added.

My sisters laughed through tears. Mike was Sarah's boyfriend. Well, technically her ex that she had broken up with months prior, though it seemed that during these tough times the two had started to hang again. He was a super nice guy and quite funny, but we're a cruel group. Once we sense a chink in the armor (i.e., you break up once), you are done. Plus he had given Sarah that hideous M&M blanket, which he had gotten for free from an internship he did at the chocolate company while he was in business school at Northeastern. Obviously he was not 'the one' for that reason alone. Sarah, two feet away from her dying father, couldn't help but let out a chuckle. Then she combed my father's hair to the side with her hand. It was a lovely gesture, which was overshadowed by Sami piling onto the joke.

"And we'll burn this dumb blanket the second we get out of here, don't worry." She was gripping a corner of the bright blue blanket like she wanted to choke the thing out.

Everyone laughed.

"Oh, you guys are sick," Pookie said, though she, too, was amused.

People in health care say a dark sense of humor is a prerequisite to getting hired. You deal with such emotionally heavy and also kinda gross stuff all day long, it's the only way to get through it. I have to agree, and I also have to boast that it's my family's finest quality. It means we can survive anything. I also think my underdeveloped emotional intelligence at the time was my best defense. If I had to relive that scene today, I would've been a mess in that hospital room. Instead, and this makes me sound like a serial killer, the intensity of the moment and the ramifications hadn't really sunk in for me yet. I knew he was dying. Fuck, I could literally see him taking his last breaths. But the past few months had been so intense and heavy and overall awful that I had grown numb to it all.

At that moment we realized his gasps for air had gotten less frequent. He took a breath, and then we waited for what felt like an eternity pass until he took another. We all got quiet knowing the next one would surely be his last. Tears began rolling down everyone's cheeks as I watched my father, my mom's husband of twenty-five years, take his last breath. Then, like a movie suddenly ending when you thought it wouldn't, his eyes closed and his mouth stayed open. It was over. He was forever in a better place.

While I want to tell you that if you haven't watched someone pass away you should, like it's some kind of amazing bucket list moment that is available on Groupon, it's not. It's weird and depressing. Before I knew it, the nurse entered, and when I looked up, she just gently gave us 'the nod.' Like, yeah... this guy isn't alive anymore. We were like, "All right, Nancy, c'mon. Show a little compassion."

It was March 22, 2002. We all gathered our things, discussed the next steps, and made sure they were going to cremate him as requested. I don't even remember how we told Natalie, who was all of eleven at the time. But I do remember she, my mom, and I piled into Pookie's coral-red Volvo V70 wagon, waved goodbye to Sarah and Sami in the parking garage, and drove home to the house I grew up in, which suddenly felt big in a negative way. As I ascended the stairs from the garage, I realized that my father would never do this ever again. He would never set foot again in that house he was so proud of finding when he decided he wanted to move back to the Boston area from a job he'd had in Maryland for six years. The house was magnificent. Four bedrooms, four baths, it was shaped like a slight V with a pull-through driveway and the Charles River running through the backyard. Woodsy trails led to a lake for pond hockey in the winter, fishing in the summer, and I had a few best friends right down the street. The interior was full of historical character like the massive front door with a peephole in it and the dumbwaiter I put the cat in once and an old racquetball court in the basement that we'd play ping-pong in on winter school nights. I had been in this house a lot without my father over the past few months, but that was because he was just fifteen miles away at a hospital. It was temporary. He'd be home at some point, I'd thought. Now he never would.

The phone was set to ring any second now. Family and friends knew we had had our heavy regroup just hours ago with my father's physician. They would be champing at the bit for an update. Natalie went to her room to grab a book to read. I entered the kitchen, lost. Should we reach out and update everyone on the news? Should we sit down and start making the proper arrangements for his wake and funeral? Grab a notepad and begin his obituary? They were all proper next steps, but not one of them sounded enjoyable to Pookie and me. So she grabbed an old-ass bottle of Chardonnay from the fridge, and I turned on HBO. The inmates were now running the asylum.

CHAPTER 3
SAYING GOODBYE WITH
BAGPIPES

I THINK a rite of passage for every adult is getting good at things no one cares about.

"I get up at six a.m. everyday. Even on weekends!"

"I can mow the grass in under an hour. Some say it takes longer but trust me, I can do it in forty-five minutes."

"I know how to make my own hummus."

At the beginning of 2002, in the middle of January while my father was in the ICU, I'd begin my training on 'the funeral circuit.' This is a fifteen-plus-year-long bender of wakes and funerals that kicked off with my grandmother's and molded me into an Olympic athlete when it came to death and dying. This is not a skill that is handed to you overnight. In fact I'm still 'training' to this day. But you must put in the work, which includes being charming or at least *passing* for charming, having an admiration for mini chicken salad sandwiches, and owning a gray or black suit.

All I owned in January 2002 were some '90s Tommy Hilfiger polos.

Mary Louise, my dad's mother, got the (death) ball rolling by going first. Over Thanksgiving she had fallen going down a step and broken her hip. She was admitted into the hospital and immediately went into withdrawal from not having alcohol readily available. She declined quickly both physically and mentally. She was also deeply afraid of outliving her son. She had lost a few babies to crib deaths when my father was young, so I think she couldn't bear to lose another child in her lifetime. Tragically understandable. She passed two months after the Turkey Day fall, in January 2002, making sure her son didn't go before her. Unfortunately for him, he couldn't really go anywhere. At least not without help.

My father's good friend Paul Doyle arranged to have an ambulance drive him and my father to my grandmother's funeral. A suave move, if not a necessary one. My father was still in and out of the ICU as well as the rehab place to help him regain feeling in his legs.

Freshly showered and standing in nothing but Gap boxers and dress socks, I stood in my father's walk-in closet, staring at over a dozen Brooks Brothers suits and amazingly colorful sports coats. Up until this point I couldn't remember the last time I had been at a funeral. All my grandparents had still been alive as of days ago. I'm sure there was a rogue great-aunt along the way that I just forgot about, but it's hard as a kid to feel the impact of those moments. You don't know the weight of death yet.

My dad had a surprising fondness for clothes. Beyond the suits he sported daily there were pieces for all occasions and activities: a white *Miami Vice*–style white blazer, yellow golf pants with little golfers all over it, one-to-three-piece suits for daytime boardroom meetings or nighttime charity events at the Children's Hospital. Then there was the weekend attire, which consisted mostly of polos. Most of these had on them either the logo for Brae Burn, his country club, or a lighthouse, belonging to the country club that never could be "his."

The lighthouse logo belonged to Sankaty Head Golf Club, a pretentious, old-money country club on Nantucket where my father always wanted to become a member. Friends that were members vouched for him. He played there at least once or twice a year with those guys, yet at the end of the day the best he could get was waitlisted. I think he even got Jack Welch, the former president of GE, to write a letter on his behalf, but it still didn't cut the Grey Poupon. The only way he was getting on the course was if a friend invited him, or if he decided to caddy again.

I grabbed a simple, gray suit off the rack and suddenly found myself transformed into Steve Martin from *Father of the Bride*.

"What's new, pussycat? Whoa, whoa! I said 'What's new, pussyca–'"

ADD is a powerful thing. I was supposed to be mourning; instead I was working the floor-length mirror like a Vegas lounge act.

Truthfully I was sad that my grandmother had passed. I didn't learn until I was fifteen that she was very abusive to my dad and his siblings growing up; with me she was extremely doting. An alcoholic throughout my dad's upbringing, she was physical, verbally demeaning, and really did a number psychologically on all her kids. She had a history I was clueless about —an affair with a man we'd call "Uncle Ollie," who, it turns out, wasn't my Uncle; running errands for Boston crime families and even serving jail time at one point; and stealing thousands of dollars from my dad and his brother. They had each tirelessly worked two jobs after school to save up for a car and my Grandmother offered to hold onto the money for them until they reached their goal, only for them to discover six months later when they were ready to buy the car that their mother had spent every last dime. But as a child, every time I saw her, she'd say to my Grandfather, "Jack, get him some money." He'd reach into his pocket and pull out some dollar bills and hand them to her. She'd shove the wad of cash into my hand to hide it and lean in and say, "This is just for you." She might've been a villain in a previous life, but to me she was family.

As we walked up to the church for the funeral service I could see my dad's ambulance pull into the back entrance. I'm saying 'my dad's ambulance' like he owned the thing and drove it to get groceries, but you know what I mean. I watched as Paul Doyle hopped out first, followed by the EMT's, who helped lower my father down in his wheelchair. I knew right then and there that what I was seeing in front of me was not new, but it was about to be for so many inside.

If you have the chance to see your father in a wheelchair as his mother's casket is wheeled by, give it a 'hard pass.'

As the casket was wheeled by us all inside, they stopped so my dad could say goodbye. We all watched as he put his hand on the casket and proceeded to cry. It was at that moment that many friends and colleagues began to gather around to see who was sitting in the wheelchair sobbing. The color drained from their faces when they realized it was Jack Colbert. If they were not welling up with tears, they were in complete shock. The last time they had seen him was probably not just two months ago, and already he was unrecognizable. Partners and staff from his law firm were used to him strutting around the fifty-some-thing-floor high-rise in downtown Boston. He didn't just work a room; he worked the whole damn building.

Now they saw a hundred-year-old-looking man bound to a wheelchair, emotional over the loss of his mother. It was a heavy sight for us all. I imagine the loss of my grandmother was a very complicated topic for Dad. She was someone who had stolen his savings as a teenager so he couldn't buy a car to get to school and work, an evil person with demons of her own, but she was still his mother. Whatever he was going through, he wore it on his sleeve that day. With Paul by his side, he was put back in 'his ambulance,' and it slowly pulled out of the church parking lot. No one wanted to say what we were all thinking.

There was no sense in fully putting these outfits away when we got home.

Three months later the time came, as we all knew it would. The good news was my father proved to everyone that he could still throw a good party. His funeral was way better than Grandmother Mary Louise's, and yes, you can rate funerals.

"There's a line out the door," Sami said.

As we stood in the funeral home for the wake, hugging and greeting friends and family as the receiving line progressed, I couldn't get over how big of a turnout my dad got.

The receiving line moved up a few people, and—"Holy shit!" I let out, at a wake, as I saw who was coming up next.

'Scotty Too Hottie', my fraternity brother's nickname, stood before me. He cracked up and nodded to everyone behind me. I looked down the line and saw twenty-plus guys from my fraternity at Keene State had driven down just for the event. These guys partied harder than Mötley Crüe yet had hearts of gold. I was touched.

This also didn't feel real. In my house with my mother, the word 'death' never really was spoken. Mom was clinging to hope so hard and fighting the good fight that I never thought my dad would actually die. I also had seen too many movies. Surely the good guy would always prevail. But funerals force people to reconnect. When they're gone and there's no more hoping left, you can celebrate. Not like that, but you can celebrate their life. It's an odd, yet beautiful thing.

At my father's wake I saw friends of his I hadn't seen in ages. My dad's sisters from Florida flew up a lot during the hospital visits, and now they were here again to say goodbye to him. I know they spent a fortune on travel that year, but I'm glad they did. A Colbert wake or funeral isn't dull. We surround ourselves with too much personality for that. I even heard my mother laugh out loud at one point. Yes, we were grieving, but there were so many good memories about my father that bonded us all that night that people couldn't help but laugh, even as a tear was still rolling down their faces.

Then there was the funeral. If people thought they got emotional at the wake, my father had a pièce de résistance lined up for the main event two days later.

A bagpipe player. Pookie had arranged it with our church when they were planning the service.

That's right. There was a goddamn bagpipe player playing outside our church as people arrived. It was like a weapon of mass destruction for people's hearts. No matter how they first heard it, it hit them.

When people parked their cars down the street and the sound of him hit, they cried.

People walking up the front path cried.

People shopping at a nearby bakery even started to cry and didn't know why.

Live music outside of your funeral is highly recommended.

The service was nicely done. I sat up front with my mother and sisters and never stopped crying. There's something educational and fascinating about death. You learn more about the deceased. You hear all their accolades. Great-Aunt Bertha painted watercolors in her attic? Fascinating. My dad was a member of the Union League? Who knew!

Back at the house the celebration of life continued. It was a beautiful, sunny spring day in New England, and no one wanted it to end. Or for the honey-baked ham to run out. At one point I stood in the corner of the kitchen just dipping slices of ham into mustard and eating them. I wasn't processing that my father had died a week ago. I was still running on autopilot. People were concerned about me and periodically would come up to me to offer their support. I weirdly just kept eating that ham. Grief makes you ravenous.

After a few hours, people started to head out. My girlfriend at the time, Sydney, had come to the service, and I was walking her back to her car when my dufus neighbor, a middle-aged man I knew mostly because I was friends with his kids, saw us as he was walking his dog. He had always seemed a bit off every time I was over at their house. Not in an alarming way, but more like he was socially clueless. Which still tracked.

"John, are you guys having a party or something?" he asked, sounding upbeat and excited.

"More like a funeral."

"Oh! Who died?"

"My dad."

I let him stand there dumbfounded as I kissed Sydney goodbye. He thought we were having our own Lollapalooza and just didn't invite him. My dad had been deathly ill for the past six months. There were two active book clubs on our street. News traveled fast in that neighborhood, but some people need to be doused in awkwardness to learn a lesson.

As I was walking back to the house, shocked by this interaction, I saw Pam Peterson walking to her car but something wasn't right. Pam, a good friend of my mom, had had too much to drink that day and for good reason. Her first husband was a cop who was killed in the line of duty his last week before retiring. So my father's funeral, and its bagpipes, brought up a lot of tough memories for her. Todd, my oldest sister's husband, was coming out the front door as Pam sidled to her car, and we locked eyes.

He mimed and mouthed to me, "She's hammered."

I intercepted Pam as she got into her Volvo sedan and started the ignition.

"Hey, Pam, can I drive you home?" I asked.

"Hi, John, that's so kind of you, but I'll be okay," Pam said.

"Why don't you just leave your car here? I'll give you a ride home, and someone can drop it off tomorrow."

"You're sweet, hon, but I'm okay."

That was when I had to bring in the big guns.

"I've been to one funeral this week, Mrs. Peterson. Don't make me go to another."

She looked at me for a moment, then slid over so I could drive. Did I feel good about what I'd said? Well, yeah. I felt like fucking Thor. It was actually a nice drive to her condo. Her car was a smooth ride, and Pam is conversational, so I loved it. Plus, I feel like I saved a life. That's a feeling that never gets old.

Later that night, after everyone had gone home, I was surveying what beer was left in the fridge when I heard Natalie doing her oddly high-pitched baby voice.

"Does Muffin want a snackie?"

I found her with the door open, leading down the basement, calling to our cat, Muffin.

"Hey, what's up?" I asked.

"Nothing," she said. "Just saw Muffin go down to eat, I think."

We got Muffin when I was eight. My parents had granted me the naming rights as long as I promised to take care of her. I think I was just really into muffins at the time. No clue how else I landed there. But Muffin was always 'my cat,' and I loved her even when she turned on me. Once, when I was snuggling with her, I stared at her and said I love you. Her paws moved in a flash and slashed my forehead. Lesson learned: Don't get in her face. My first foray into how to properly treat a woman. Aside from that, Muffin was a cutie and could be a good snuggler, as long as it was on her terms.

So now Natalie was calling down to our cat in the basement because, in the past two years, as an older cat Muffin had come to love hanging out in the basement. It was where her litter box was, and it was cooler down there during the humid, summer months. She went down there so much that when she did pass away that following summer, just three months after my dad, some people in the house didn't exactly notice that she had died. Specifically Natalie, who was just twelve, and diagnosed with a nonverbal learning disability and legally blind in her left eye. When my mom asked Natalie if she knew where Muffin was, Natalie snapped that she was "in the basement, geez!"

My mother and I looked at one another like we had just dodged a bullet. "Okay, just checking," Pookie replied.

Sometimes the truth takes too much work.

On the day of Dad's funeral, Natalie and I stood at the top of the basement stairs, unaware that we'd only have a few more months with Muffin, and we chuckled at her love for that creepy basement. In her defense she was probably so old and so uncomfortable that that was the only place she could escape from us jackasses and get some sense of relief. That was when I heard a noise in the office.

I left Natalie to go find Pookie standing over the pool table in my father's office, opening up the mail. People always wonder what you do during times like this, when just hours earlier you were listening to bagpipes at your husband's funeral. Do you sit and stare at the wall? Do you follow Pam's lead and chug a bottle of merlot? You have to understand, though, that my father's cancer had been a six-year ordeal. We had had time to mentally prepare, and I've learned from Pookie that you can still go about your daily life during hard times. The distractions can help.

As I entered the room, Mom huffed to herself. "You gotta be fucking kidding me."

"What?" I said.

She flipped the letter around, and I spotted the lighthouse logo immediately.

She began to read out loud: "Dear Jack, it is with great pleasure that we announce your acceptance into the Sankaty Head Golf Club."

My dad finally got into that stupid country club on Nantucket.

They say the secret to great comedy is timing. We chuckled for a moment. What else could you do in the face of something so insane? But I could feel that the same part of my brain that emitted laughter was also ready to emit sobbing. At that moment I chose to let one take the spotlight over the other.

Eventually, I wouldn't have a choice.

STAGE 2: OBSESS OVER THE PAST

Time to go down memory lane b*tch!

CHAPTER 4
THERE ONCE WAS A MAN FROM NANTUCKET

IT MIGHT BE gross to start off a chapter about my father with the first line from a pervy limerick, but as Outback Steakhouse says, "No rules, just right." Besides, I think it's important to go back in time before my father was full of cancer and Sankaty was still a pipe dream. In 1981, when I was just a baby in Pookie's arms, my parents toured the island of Nantucket, looking for an investment property. Realistically they were looking for 'a place to escape our nutjob parents and the sweaty 'burbs of Boston.' My mom actually gets credit for discovering the island for us. She nannied there one summer when she was seventeen. Then, years after, she met my father, and right around the time I had just graced their world with my presence, my dad probably said, "Cher, a beach house would be a good investment for us." Then she said, "Jackie baby, I know just the place!"

In all seriousness this is how they talked when they were in a good mood. Just imagine my mom doing a dorky dance while delivering her line and my father slurring his words during his.

KIDDING! He drank moderately, contrary to his Irish Catholic upbringing.

They bought a modest three-bedroom house on the south-western side of the island, which is known as Tom Nevers. According to Pookie, they had to take out a loan that was so large it was terrifying, but back in 1981 you could still buy a house on Nantucket for less than a billion dollars, so life was pretty great. I'd like to think I helped them find the house, but in reality I probably lay in my mother's arms all day, filling my diaper and snoring. I'm still really good at one of those things. You decide which one.

I have great pride when it comes to my parents having a Nantucket house when they were in their thirties, especially because of their upbringing. As I've mentioned, my father had an insanely abusive mother: she stole his savings, was a raging alcoholic, and he grew up in Dorchester, a tough part of Boston at the time. Pookie didn't have it any easier. Her dad was a misogynist who didn't offer my mom a dime for college, and when Pookie's youngest brother, Chuckie, was seventeen, he died in a tragic accident while 'playing' with a gun with friends. These lovebirds grew up in tough households, then worked their crotches off so their kids wouldn't know what that was like.

Nantucket is an extremely special place for me. We would go for two weeks every summer when I was a kid and rent it out for the remainder of the summer to help pay for it. I have a lot of great memories there. I was either on my little BMX bike, riding up and down the street with new friends I'd made, on the beach jumping in waves, or up at the house, working on some arts and crafts. On Nantucket I was like a creative prodigy. I could draw, make friendship bracelets, or even put together a goddamn model ship. Then I'd get back on the mainland and drool and talk like a caveman while watching *The Sword in the Stone* for the fiftieth time. The island does something magical to you in the sense that you don't feel the need to watch TV. Shocking, I know.

It also did something occasionally that was appealing to my parents, but not a fifteen-year-old boy. Make that two of them. One Columbus Day weekend, my parents and I went to check on the house before closing it up for the winter. They let me bring my good friend Brian, which was fun. We were each reading in our twin beds one night, when we started to hear a creaking sound coming from my parents' bedroom. Our beds, separated by an antique side table, were stacked head to toe. As if on cue, we slowly took our eyes off our books and exchanged the same nervous expression. The creaking increased. Brian slowly slunk down to bury his head under his comforter. As if that beach-themed bedspread could muffle the gross passion coming from the master bedroom. In case we had a hint of uncertainty as to what the source of the sounds was, the next morning confirmed it. As I walked down the stairs all groggy I was greeted by a gameshow host.

"HEYYY, JOHNNY BOY! COME ON DOWN. WHO WANTS EGGS?!" my father yelled with so much enthusiasm. He was sporting an apron and a smile so large it was my first time seeing it. He began spooning out scrambled eggs onto plates. "There's fresh juice on the table."

Gross.

The eggs were phenomenal, though.

What I liked about my dad was that he wasn't perfect. He

was a city boy who was cursed with flat, narrow feet and a workaholic mindset. He grew up playing sports but always had more than one job, which he juggled with school. For someone who was amazingly coordinated in the world of business, he could be astoundingly the opposite in the world of athleticism. I'm psyched I only inherited his beautiful flat feet and not his math skills. Thanks for that, Pops.

Take the time we drove out to Great Point when I was about thirteen to surf-cast and barbeque as a family. We did the cool thing where you deflate your tires (you have no choice), then put the '89 Montero in four-wheel drive and drove out onto the beachy strip of sand that goes from the main, beefy part of Nantucket all the way out to the Q-tip-looking, farthest northeastern point known as Great Point. As you drive along, with the ocean about fifty yards away on either side of you, you feel like you're in a Diane Lane movie and suddenly wild horses are gonna gallop by with a shirtless Richard Gere on one of them. That's how picturesque it is. And the fact that once you get there a massive, old, white lighthouse known as the Great Point Lighthouse serves as your beacon for where to park doesn't hurt either.

Was it a beautiful day to be a Colbert? You bet your ass it was. It was also great to be a son. Every father-and-son duo in New England was out there that day surf casting their hearts out into what felt like the ends of the Earth. (The term 'surf casting' means you cast your line into the sea from either the shore or near the shore. You're barefoot on the sand as the water washes up to your shins, or, if the water is calm, you're standing in it up to your knees.) My dad was on cloud nine in his yellow, cable-knit 1992 Tommy Hilfiger sweater with a polo underneath as he and I cast out. We were full of happiness as waves crashed and the mist from them hit us in the face. It didn't even faze us that neither of our lines got one bite. We were both genuinely having a good time surf casting and felt like, in the game of life, we got points just for showing up.

"Whoo, this water is cold but feels good!" my dad shouted over the waves crashing at a safe distance.

"I know," I replied in my cliché, less-is-not-more tween way.

"Maybe we should get a little closer so our lures go out farther, like the other guys?" he yelled.

Saltwater slapped him in the face, yet his smile didn't flinch. It was like he was having a good time that day, no matter what. He inched forward in the shin-high water, now not so safely far away from the crashing waves. I looked around and stopped as I noticed two guys actually both reeling things in just down the beach. I had been 100 percent confident that the fish just weren't biting that night at Great Point and it had nothing to do with our skill set... until I saw stupid Chad and Brooks, both tanked off Heineken, catching bluefish like pros.

I had just turned back in the direction of my dad with a frown on my face from my new reality check when he did something pretty impressive. Dad had now advanced about twenty feet farther into the ocean than our original spot and had pulled off casting from it. He casted and reeled in twice before another set of waves came in. It was on his third cast that I think the tides literally switched from low to high, and the first wave to clock in was like, "I got the fifty-year-old man in the Hilfiger polo." The moment my dad rotated his torso and cast that line out, you could hear the twing of the line as it flew out from the reel just before you heard five thousand gallons of saltwater take the shape of a wave and low-key murder my father. The wave didn't so much crash down over his head as it did steam roll him into oblivion. If they had been that big before he waded out, he wouldn't have risked standing there. That's what was so deceiving about this small overachiever of a wave we'll call "Rudy." It was like tit-level, but its grandmother must've been a tsunami because that thing came in low and slow and didn't stop until my dad was on the floor. He went face-first into the surf, catching himself with his hands so the water was up to his elbows. By the time Rudy got to me, it was like a cute little ripple. The state of my frown at this point? That thing was a full-blown smile, possibly emitting some uncontrollable laughter. My dad's chipper, preppy cable-knit sweater? Soaked to the bone.

Twenty minutes later I was reading on the beach by my family's car when I heard "Chad" and "Brooks" walking back to their cars. They couldn't stop laughing.

"Did you see the guy that got nailed?" one muttered with amusement to his buddy.

"How could I not? He got soaked! Why was he dressed so nicely?"

Were they talking about some other middle-aged father that got hit by a crashing wave while surfing? Nope. How do I know? Because they turned around, saw my dad following behind them, and when they faced forward, they chuckled again. But what was great about Jack Colbert is when I told him what happened, he died laughing. He wasn't pissed. He was soaked, that's for damn sure, but he couldn't stop laughing about it.

He even asked me to do the impression of them later that night.

"What did the guys say again?" my dad asked with a smile as he was packing the car up to head home.

I then did my best Chad and Brooks impressions, reciting their lines while my father laughed and laughed. I know some dads that would've been dropping f-bombs left and right and been pissy the rest of the day if that had happened to them, but my dad? He loved it. He didn't care that he didn't catch one fish. He was just happy that he was able to do that on a Tuesday. He also could see how comical it was that he got nailed while being overdressed for surfcasting. The only part that was annoying was I had to keep doing the "Chad and Brooks" impressions at every dinner party we went to for the rest of that trip. My dad was like a little kid that just kept saying, "Do it again!" Fortunately for him I feed off laughs, so I'd shrug and do it for the twentieth time, pretending like it was the first.

CHAPTER 5
MY NUMBER ONE FAN

SUPERMAN. Wonder Woman. Steven Seagal. Heroes take many forms. Mine took on the shape of a forty-ish white man wearing a polo and two chins. When I was eight years old, my dad put himself on the line for me in a way that will go down in history. He didn't save me from a burning building or give me his kidney. He did something far more daring and original. He gave me a gift that was exciting to a son and repulsive to a mother.

It was the summer of 1989. We were on Nantucket, and we started the night at Vincent's Restaurant with another family that we'd known and vacationed with for years. It's no longer around, but that was a gem of a restaurant for, like, twenty-five years. I even was a bartender there the summer before junior year of college. But on this particular night I was very much under the age of twenty-one and overstuffed from a big meal with my immediate family and our friends. We then did what we did any time we had the privilege of going into town at night: we window-shopped. This routine consisted of sauntering up Main Street and looking in the windows, admiring things like Bass boat shoes at the Nobby Shop or popping into the Nantucket Pharmacy for a $1.29 cone of ice cream. (This place was phenomenal. It was an old ice cream parlor that also sold stuff like sunscreen and balsa-wood planes. Then there was a pharmacy in the back for when you needed gallons of cortisone cream after trampling through poison ivy, which grew all over the island.)

On this very night, things went a little differently. Maybe it was the perfect seventy-two-degree Nantucket weather that made us decide to window-shop longer than usual. Or maybe it was the fact that all the adults were pretty tipsy from multiple bottles of Italian wine. Either way, on that unicorn of a night, we happened to pass by a T-shirt store that had a little something special in its window. Not only did it have sweatshirts, but this shop had racy tees as well. Which was rare. The usual tone of the dozens of tourist shops on Nantucket is either cool, sweetly punny, or heartfelt. This was edgier than that. It was like Spencer Gifts: Beach Town Edition.

One specific T-shirt caught everyone's eye.

"Does that shirt say, 'Who farted?" I asked, amazed to learn such a thing existed.

You read that correctly. It was a basic white tee with "WHO FARTED?" printed on the top in an obnoxious, black font. Beneath that headline was a cartoon scene of a room full of animals and plants who had allegedly died from someone's really bad gas. The dog was on its back with all four legs up in the air and *x*'s over his eyes; every plant was flopped over in its pot, lifeless. The bird in the cage? Dead. The goldfish in the fishbowl? That's right, super dead. There were black, squiggly lines to illustrate gassy fumes all over the room, which really tied the piece together nicely.

Everyone was dying laughing except for one person.

Pookie.

"If you buy him that shirt you are sleeping on the couch!" she told my father.

"I AM GETTING JOHN THAT SHIRT!" my dad exclaimed. "I mean, look at it! It's perfect!"

I turned around in shock and excitement to see my dad was clapping and praising the universe for introducing him to such a novelty item that he felt was perfect for his only son. Toilet humor was my specialty. He knew this. I knew this. Heck, the other family we were with knew this. But Pookie wasn't convinced. The T-shirt was super distasteful, and she would have to answer to fellow friends and family for this. And worse. To other moms.

Everyone's heads were swiveling back and forth between Jack and Cheryl to see who would win this prize fight. Unfortunately for my mother, my dad wasn't backing down. It's like he let her win so many arguments over the years just so he could be a stubborn son of a bitch on this one showdown. He had so much heart for this fart shirt Pookie didn't stand a chance.

"Look at the dog!" my dad said, giggling. "It's out cold!"

My mother just pursed her lips and shook her head. I think she even walked away, not caring where she was going; anywhere away from that discussion would have been better in her mind. I'm not really sure. Meanwhile, my father, some of our family friends, and I were huddled around my dad at the register as he put his marriage on thin ice with a simple flick of a pen on the sales receipt.

For the rest of the summer and all through the next twelve months, I wore that shirt with pride. It's allure had worn off so much that after the first week that I'd forget I was wearing it until people would point and laugh at it. It's kinda like a mustache. Guys will give you a head nod out of respect; women will look away with disgust. That's what the "WHO FART-ED?" shirt was like.

We'll never know who in the illustrated image farted per se, but we do know this: my father risked divorce over a $22 fart shirt for his son. Talk about standing up for what you believe in. That man locked into his goal and didn't waver when the odds or, in this case, his wife, gave him opposition. As Sean Connery says in the nineties blockbuster *The Rock*, "Losers do their best. Winners go home and fuck the prom queen." Or, in this case, they go home and sleep on the very far edge of the queen bed with a terrific ocean breeze and one eye open.

The summer before my junior year of college, I returned to Nantucket to work, but this time I took on two jobs. Nantucket was great because it was the only place I know of that you could pull this off without your multiple employers getting pissy at one another. I was to return to my previous summer job, the Nantucket Health Club, and then I got a new job as the service bartender at Vincent's. Yes, there are other restaurants on the island. This was just the only one that was cool with me serving booze at the ripe old age of twenty.

I've never regretted working two jobs that summer. The only regret I have is how I acted the night my father came in to Vincent's to eat by himself during one of my shifts. I remember it like it was yesterday. The hostess sat him at the nice little table up front, in the picture window that overlooks South Water Street. The little service bar where I worked had a direct line of sight down the middle of all the tables, so from my vantage point I could see the entire first floor of tables, including the one at the front, where my father was now seated. He waved to me; I smiled and waved back.

"Who's that?" his waitress asked me.

Kind of embarrassed, I said, "That's my dad."

"Aw, that's nice," she said with a big smile and proceeded to bring him ice water and the menu.

That waitress was a sweetheart. Once I uttered "my dad," she went into full Momma Bird mode. She refilled his wine glass every chance she could get while my father sat there, contentedly people-watching like the pro that he was. And what did I do? I came over for a second to say hi. Maybe sixty seconds; not even two minutes.

I was twenty. I had no idea that in four months they'd find all those tumors. Much less that in another three months he'd pass away.

This is when the bag full of regret starts to overflow.

I didn't appreciate my father. He came over to the bar with a good-natured chuckle and said I had to be careful, they had given him so much wine. He even said he had leftovers he would put in the fridge for me when I got home. I was nice but not chatty enough. Not chatty enough with my only dad who, in a year, would be dead. He was always around, and at that time I figured he'd be around forever. What was the big deal?

The big deal is that you can lose someone instantly. I know I shouldn't regret things like, Why didn't I tell my boss I was taking a break and join my father for ten minutes at his little table? Why didn't I act more fun when he came in in general? He was proud to see me working there, but besides some small talk throughout the night, given the impersonal way I acted, he could have been my high school chemistry teacher for all my bosses knew.

Now, in my forties, I know how differently I would act if this happened in the present day. I would've had him sit near my station so we could chat the entire night. I would've drunk with him because screw that job. At the time I took it so seriously and was cranky half the time from working too much and not knowing what I was doing. That night I focused on the wrong thing. There's nothing I can do about it now, but it's a moment amongst many that I regret when I look back on the last few years I had with my father.

⌐

A year after my father's death, in the spring of 2003, my three sisters, my mother, and I all traveled to Nantucket to honor my father's wishes. He wanted to have his ashes scattered off the bluff in our backyard in Tom Nevers, overlooking the Atlantic Ocean. It was a romantic request—not to mention challenging.

While town can be a beautifully hot eighty-two degrees on that island, Tom Nevers is not. Its southeastern location on the island makes it vulnerable to cooler temps and strong winds. This is also why it happens to be the most relaxing place on Earth. You can be sweating like a pig in Boston, but when you get to the house three hours later, you're marveling at the ocean air coming through the living room windows, bringing your core temp down thirty degrees like some sort of witchcraft. It's why "That ocean air!" is a constant catchphrase in my family. It's what we blame for not being able to keep our eyes open past eight p.m. and why the house was playfully named 'Windswept.' Yes, everyone obnoxiously names their house on the island. At least ours wasn't a pun, thank god.

Which brings me back to that spring. Just like my father had been in life, the bag of his ashes sat still, sealed inside his silver urn on the kitchen counter, while the five of us scurried around Windswept to get our shoes and coats on. I don't know, it's not like these ashes had to be spread at a specific time. We're just anxious nutjobs.

"Do I need a jacket?" Sarah yelled from a bedroom.

"Maybe grab a fuzzy!" Sami and I yelled jokingly. This was a term Pookie had coined years earlier for a fleece. Given a long leash, the woman basically adds a 'y' or 'ie' to anything. Fuzzies, jammies, you get the idea.

Moments later we were all assembled in the kitchen. Some of us were ready to cry. Most of us looked like we're about to rake leaves.

As we headed out to the bluff, I don't remember the wind being its usual cantankerous self. If it had been, we would have postponed. The sun was out, and there was just a light breeze here and there–not enough to concern us, but enough to set the tone for a spiritual moment between our family and this place my father had loved so much.

My mom, my three sisters, and I all stood along the bluff overlooking Tom Nevers Beach. It was pure sand and the

Atlantic Ocean. There was not a soul in sight, nor a damn clue as to what we should say.

"Sooooo," Sami joked.

"Here, I'll start," Pookie said, holding the urn. "Jack... we love you, and, umm..." She laughed. She didn't know what to say either.

Sarah, the most in tune with her emotions, chimed in.

"Dad, we love you. Now you're in your favorite spot, and we hope to make you proud." She started to get emotional, though, and took a break.

I was ready to join her in Emo City. Everything was lining up perfectly for an epic cry sesh. The sun was over the beautiful horizon. My father's ashes were about to be spread at his favorite place on Earth. Cue up the *The Last of the Mohicans* soundtrack, and it would've been game over for me.

"Should I?" Pookie looked at all of us, then at the urn. We nodded and lightly chuckled, like nervous kids at a school dance.

I braced myself for the tears that were about to fire out of my eye sockets.

Pookie braced herself, about to spread ashes in slow motion like Mother Teresa. Ever so gently, she cocked her wrist and proceeded to shake some ashes out. Only they didn't sprinkle out. They hit the open air and the Nantucket trade winds like a bat out of hell.

Suddenly I was in pain. "Ugh, my eye!" I yelped.

My father was no longer present just in spirit, but in ash too.

"Whoops," Pookie said matter-of-factly as some ash stuck to her sleeve.

"It's too windy. Here, Mom, let me try," Sami said as she took the reins. She did the same thing: got all strategic with her ash sprinkling, only to have it fly back at her like a boomerang. We all took turns trying our 'methods' because even though we saw the person next to us fail, we thought, *Must be their form.* The truth was we were outnumbered against the breezy bluff. Ashes were now flying all over the place, covering our shoes, our clothes, even hitting us straight in the face.

"OH MY GOD!" we all started yelling while trying not to laugh. An open mouth would be unfortunate with ashes in the air. I made a break for the house, and soon, the others followed. Now safely standing behind a sliding glass door, where no remains could get us, we looked out at the incredible view. The sun was beaming down on the horizon. The eelgrass on the bluff was swaying harshly in the wind. And our father's ashes were so spread out it was impossible to tell if we had honored his wish successfully. He was now on the bluff... as well as the shrubs, some outdoor furniture, and a few of our neighbors' houses. But the urn was empty, so technically we did our job. It's not our fault my dad, who knew the bluff could often be windy, didn't take that into consideration when he asked to be spread off of it! Or maybe he did and wanted one last laugh from the heavens.

What has comforted me and my siblings and the Pookster all these years later is that, no matter what happens with Windswept, my father will be there forever.

CHAPTER 6

PAKE BITTS

GROWING up we would periodically go on vacations to places other than our beach house on Nantucket. If it involved a flight, it was usually a work trip, where my dad was attending a conference and we were staying at a swanky hotel. He shoved us all in the same room to save money and to also check the box on family fun.

One trip stood out above the rest, maybe because it wasn't for work. Or maybe because it's where a nickname was born that is still alive to this day.

In August 2001, we took a family trip to Jackson Hole, Wyoming. If you've never heard of Jackson Hole, it's like Aspen, Colorado's late-blooming cousin. It's got a charming town center, Yellowstone National Park, the Grand Tetons, and Harrison Ford. (He has a ranch there and literally saves climbers with his helicopter. FYI we never once saw Harrison or Calista the entire time we were there. It was bullshit.)

At the time of our trip my father was a few rounds in on his cancer treatment and still going strong. Radiation was going well, so his spirits were high, as were his standards.

"Damn it, she did it again," he barked as we stood outside the Hertz rental car center thirty miles from Jackson Hole.

"Who, Barbara?" my mom chimed in. Negativity is to Mom as chum is to sharks. She can smell a drop of it a mile away.

My three sisters, and my now brother-in-law, Todd, and I all stood around our luggage, clueless. Had iPhones been invented, we would've been on them. Instead we had to stand by the car that had been reserved for us: some sort of wagon or minivan, a vehicle I was quickly learning just wouldn't suffice.

"Yes, Barbara, my secretary," Dad replied. "We can't all fit in that." He gestured toward the poor car sitting in front of us. It sat parked in its assigned parking space at F22 ashamed, like some indoor kid who's been picked last for kickball. We could all fit in the same hotel room just fine, but packed into a modest minivan? You gotta be kidding me.

"She's just not following through like she used to," he quipped as he headed for the rental office.

Moments later we were sitting in the largest vehicle ever to be issued for civilians–the Ford Excursion. It's the Grand Tetons of SUVs, with its forty-five rows of seating and horrible gas mileage. But most importantly it fit all seven of us and our dumb suitcases, so my father, and now all of us, were quite content as we headed to our hotel.

←

. . .

On our way to a white water rafting excursion the next day, my father made an announcement: "I think I should have a nickname."

Everyone cracked up. Natalie did, too, not because she got the humor but because she was little and wanted to keep up with her intense family.

My sister Sami was one of the first to perk up with curiosity. "What kind of nickname?" she asked.

"There's a character in the book I'm reading. He's a cowboy," Dad says with 70 percent confidence and 30 percent fear we were going to think he was crazy. The book he was referring to was *Close Range: Wyoming Stories* by Annie Proulx. My father came across it when he was doing research months prior to this trip. I wasn't used to him diving so deep into reference material prior to a trip. But this one was special because it was a true vacation he'd been looking forward to for a while and I think deep down he knew that with the side effects of his prostate cancer battle such as his overactive bladder and incontinence–he wouldn't be able to travel like this forever.[1]

We were all still taken aback by this nickname thing. Where did the desire come from? Maybe it was because friends of my parents were now getting dumb nicknames like Pee-Pop and May-May from their grandkids. Sami did get pregnant with my nephew, Tyler, the following year, so maybe my dad sensed a grandkid was on the way and he wanted to be ready with his special nickname that he could repeat in a baby voice

---

1. I borrowed his car to get groceries once and noticed a pack of adult diapers in the trunk. I brought it up and we joked about it but that was one of the first times where I realized my dad was not immortal and truly getting older right in front of me. It was a bit of a shock to the system.

until his grandkids said it naturally. Or maybe it was just because he was really gravitating toward this new found cowboy lifestyle. Riding horses, firing guns, and, of course, the urban cowboy activity: white-tablecloth dining, dry-aged sirloin, and a fantastic glass of red wine

Whatever his reasoning, we were all aboard the emotional ship he was steering and instantly wanted to hear more.

"This is so weird. What's the cowboy's name?" I shouted from the thirtieth row of the Excursion.

Everyone starting shouting out cliché names like Hoss and Billy. They even did bad cowboy impressions. When the hurricane of verbal diarrhea subdued, my father responded.

"Pake Bitts."

"Pake *Bitts*?" my mother asked. "What kind of name is Pake Bitts?"

Everyone was amused, but also into it.

"Do we just call you Pake?" my brother-in-law, Todd, asked.

My dad nodded with a smile. We all laughed. We were on vacation in Jackson f*cking Hole, Wyoming, and my dad's cancer had ghosted him for the summer. If his Make-A-Wish request was to be called Pake instead of Jack, then Pake it was.

We all looked out the windows at the beautiful landscape flanking both sides of the highway, content and at peace with our current situation.

"I want a nickname too," Mom suddenly said, like a small field mouse in the corner.

"Oh god," my sisters said in surround sound, half joking. "Like Dad's?"

"I don't know, maybe," she said, sixty going on sixteen.

Normally we'd all have given her awful suggestions, but I think everyone was still in their euphoric state of reflection, too calm to be our normally rude selves.

"Any ideas? You can't really just give yourself a nickname. It's supposed to be given by others," stated Sarah, always the rule follower.

"Your father just did," she smartly replied. The woman had a point.

"Fine. Mom, what do you want your nickname to be?" Sami asked.

"I don't know. Like... Pookie?" my mom shyly replied without making eye contact. She didn't have to look around to read the room. She could hear it. We were all dying of laughter. The jury was unanimous. "Pookie," as far as a nickname went, was so random, sudden, and silly. How could we *not* approve it? It's funny when you admire a person–"Good job, Pookie!"– and still funny when you can't stand them: "God damn it, Pookie!" We were sold.

My father later explained that he wanted to have cowboy courage to help him in his fight against cancer. I think he was truthfully terrified of not being around forever. A name like Pake Bitts helped him take on an alternate persona, one that was resilient, had skin like old leather to weather the storms, and could say cool things like, "Been there, done that–bowlegged!"

My mother, on the other hand, just wanted a cute nickname so she wouldn't feel left out.

"PAKE AND POOKIE!" Todd roared with giddy laughter. And just like that, It was settled.

· · ·

Jack Colbert had a great characteristic when traveling. Well, it wasn't just one; it was more like two personality traits that were great on their own and even better combined.

First, he was charming. He knew how to make a stranger on an elevator chuckle and who exactly to slip a cash tip to, someone who deserved it but maybe wasn't expecting it. That old school way to thank someone for giving you a baller table or the best chairs at the hotel pool, or rushing a much needed drink over to you when you're an overwhelmed parent. There's something about handing someone a cash tip that feels very mafioso. I highly recommend it. The recipient will feel the same way.

Jack Colbert was also adventurous. He embraced YOLO before Drake coined it. A trip with him wasn't, "Let's fly five hours to just sit by the pool." It was more like, "What exceptional activities can we do there that we can't do in the suburbs of Massachusetts?"

I watched both of these skills play out right before my very eyes for years. I didn't realize what it was doing to me, but the training was priceless. It's how I pulled off taking a private Muay Thai lesson in Bali– and afterwards knew how to take care of the hotel waiter who brought me lavender-scented towels by the pool when my knees and feet look like they got murdered– while the other guests barely would even mutter "thank you" to the staff.

A vacation with my father was always fun yet busy. On Nantucket he would relax more in between projects, but if a flight was involved, he was going to plan the shit the out of that itinerary. He was going to do cool activities that the other lame families at the hotels wouldn't think or dare to do.

Like firing guns.

On the same Jackson Hole trip we took when I was nine-teen, one day at breakfast my father announced an idea he was excited about.

"We should go to a gun range!" he proclaimed.

My mother literally did a double take, then began to fidget with anxiety.

"That'd be fun!" Todd said, and my sister Sarah agreed. I only nodded because I had a mouth full of steak and eggs, but I would've said, "Hell yeah," if I could have. I had been really into weapons since learning about them in history classes over the years, and no, my weapons obsession wasn't dangerous. I was really into medieval weapons especially– King Arthur, Robin Hood–you know, old, rusty weapons. None of this sketchy AK-47 shit.

Moments later the concierge had a dorky, white family charging toward her desk all sporting freshly bought merch from one of the multiple hotel gift shops we had hit so far. I had a Jackson Hole hat with a moose logo on it while Sarah was sporting a bright orange, long-sleeve shirt that had the Grand Tetons on the back. Style wasn't exactly our forte. It was also 2001.

"How may I help you?" the concierge asked in a way that may have been either enthusiastic or scared.

"We wanna fire guns like cowboys!" my father blurted out. "Unfortunately, I'm not kidding," he joked.

It worked. The concierge chuckled, though her laughter had a hint of fakeness to it. Most likely her mind started to recall other jobs she could've taken. Anything would've been better than this.

Still amused, and chock-full of amazing customer service, she took the bait. "You mean like today?"

We all laughed. My brother-in-law stepped forward to help land the plane, seeing as my mom, who at the moment was anxiety with legs, was standing by my dad's side and definitely not into this plan.

"Sorry, we've all had a lot of coffee," Todd said. "Is there a shooting range or an excursion that offers that?"

A pregnant pause. The concierge waited, thinking we were still kidding. We still were not.

"Good question! Let me just see!" She proceeded to pull out a map and spotted something. "Ah yes, looks like there's one right here." She pointed to a spot a few miles from where we stood. Then she looked up at all of us to make sure we were satisfied and possibly would leave her alone now. We were all still staring at the map, clueless, and she could tell. In a graceful movement she grabbed a Daffy Duck pen from her desk and clicked the top to engage it.

"And they let you just show up and shoot rifles?" someone in my gang asked, as she circled the shooting range with her Daffy Duck pen on the unfolded map.

"Sure do!" she said without looking up as she proceeded to draw our driving route.

Twenty minutes later our party, minus my mother and Natalie, pulled up to the gun range. A few men were unloading rifles from the gun rack in the back of their pickup. Thank god Pookie wasn't with us because she would've locked the doors and not let us exit the vehicle.

We did exit the vehicle, though, because our chaperone for the day was my father.

"This is gonna be great!" he said, draped in his yellow Tommy Hilfiger polo, Nantucket Rainbow Fleet belt, and khaki shorts.

Radio silence. After Todd closed the last car door all we could hear were birds and the rapid blast of rounds being fired off on the outdoor gun range.

Something wasn't right, though. There was no one to greet us. To ask us how many guns we wanted to rent or how much ammunition we wanted to purchase. Or to even walk us through the proper safety precautions when firing off rounds from a deadly weapon. So we stood there, me, Sarah, the newly dubbed Pake Bitts, Sami, and Todd, while a few locals at their own stations just stared at us. There were no ugly looks. Just confused facial expressions.

We slowly started to figure out why.

"Jackson Hole Gun Club. Established for over 100 years," Sarah read out loud from the sign hanging overhead as we climbed up the few wooden stairs to the range.

"Excuse me," my father asked a man who looked like ZZ Top. He wore a flannel tucked into his Carhartt jeans. "Where do we rent the guns?"

"You don't. This is a private range. You have to bring your own." He smiled politely, then headed to the skeet shooting area.

My father turned around to us.

"Whoops," Todd said and we all cracked up.

Daffy Duck Pen had sent us to a private gun club. Probably not on purpose, but rather because no stupid yuppie family before us had ever visited it and reported back that it was private.

"What do we do now?" I asked in my usual I'm-nineteen-and-stupid cadence.

"Guess we can't shoot guns today," my father muttered, defeated.

That's when an angel with the body of a wine barrel appeared before us.

"Heard you folks want to shoot some guns," the stocky, kind man said as he approached us with his son trailing behind. The dad was about five-foot-eight with a sweet mustache that he didn't have to be trendy. He shook my father's hand and introduced himself. "Hank Henderson. I'd be happy to let you folks shoot some of my guns."

My father's face lit up. "Seriously? My name is Jack Colbert." He then introduced all of us.

"Of course," Hank said. "The more I can educate people on gun safety, the less likely they'll take away guns for hunters such as myself. See, Wyoming wants us to use mace when we encounter a bear, but that shit just doesn't work!"

Sarah and I exchanged a quick look.

Hank wasn't done. "What really makes a bear run away is this." He reached behind his back and pulled a .45 revolver from a holster attached to his belt at his lower back. The thing was the size of a frying pan.

"OH MY GOD," my dad said and cracked up.

"Billy," Hank said, "go get boxes of ammo from the truck for the .22, .45, and the rifle."

His son ran off like he was fetching milk for supper. Hank turned to us and flashed a grin that I'll never forget, panning around to make sure all five of us saw it. "Now let's go fire some fucking guns."

Hank was a selfless hero. We had known the man for all of thirty seconds, and he let us fire off no clue how much it cost but must've been a ton of ammo. He took the time with each of us, one by one, to show us how to properly fire the .22 pistol and the single-shot rifle. He even let Sami fire the Colt .45. After she fired one shot, the kickback was so strong she lost control of her arms and suddenly was aiming directly overhead at the wooden awning. Hank quickly came in and by the shoulders guided her to keep the gun pointed toward the range and nowhere else.

After an hour or so of playing with Hank's guns, my father dug out some cash and did the only thing he felt he should do. He shook Hank's hand, thanked him profusely, and when Hank pulled his hand away there was fifty dollars in it. He tried to give it back, but my father wouldn't let him. We owed this man much more than that for the ammo, not to mention his thoughtfulness to make sure our day turned out to be as fun as we had hoped.

As we headed to our car all on a high from the day's fun activity, Hank called after us. "Remember, when people want to ban guns, now you know they ain't so bad!"

We all laughed at his comment and turned back to our car. Hank was awesome. Our savior. Our teacher. And I'll always be grateful for that day that he gave us, especially as I look back on the fun times with my father. But Hank's an idiot if thinks any random person should be allowed to buy an assault rifle.

. . .

"Let's get tattoos," my dad said as we were driving back to the hotel days later.

"Are you drunk?" I replied as best I could without sounding like a total asshole.

"No! But wouldn't that be fun?" He was serious.

I had always thought of getting a tattoo at some point in my life. Plus, like the Pake Bitts thing, I was thoroughly entertained by the hilarious transformation my father had taken ever since we landed in Wyoming days prior. It was as if the Brooks-Brothers-suit-wearing Jack was no longer around. Pake Bitts was. And god damn it, Pake wanted a tattoo.

"Like a four-leaf clover since we're Irish?" I replied.

"I don't know," he said as if he was a little bummed he didn't have the perfect answer on the tip of his tongue. But then we came to a stoplight.

"That!" He pointed to the car in front of us as it slowed to a stop. "On the license plate."

"The bucking bronco," I said matter-of-factly. Like it was so simple. The answer to my dad's dilemma. I'm sure a lot of middle-aged men have that problem. You have a cowboy nick-name; you've been firing guns and riding horses all week. Now you just need a tattoo. But which one?

My dad turned to me and announced it like he was declaring Tuesday nights were now strictly for tacos. "If I were to get a tattoo, I'd get that. The Wyoming State symbol." Which, to clarify–because it's everywhere in that state and rightfully so–is an image of a cowboy holding on as a bronco horse tries to buck him off. It's got a great "buck up or shut up!"

vibe to it. It was not just motivational; it screamed from the Grand Tetons my dad's new persona.

"That's cool. I'd get that," I said. I then turned to look out the window and the two of us drove the rest of the way to the hotel in a peaceful silence, both content with how that tattoo convo had started and ended, all within the lifespan of about four minutes.

The truth is we never got around to getting those tattoos on that trip. So much was jam-packed in every day that it easily fell to the wayside. But what did I do after my dad's funeral? I drove my mom's friend Pam home because she was hammered. Okay, so not literally right after his funeral, but a year later, a week after I graduated from college, I printed out a photo of the bucking bronco cowboy and headed to Vermont.

Tattoos can be peaceful or polarizing. Some are discreet while others are about as subtle as a shotgun. Even the word can scream 'trashy' or 'hot' depending on the design of the tats and the body they're on. I went to college in New Hampshire circa 2002, so I saw my fair share of barbed-wire bicep tattoos and tramp stamps. But sometimes an individual will have a marking on their body that means something. Something other than, "Well, yeah, I mean, I really love guacamole. Why wouldn't I get an avocado tattooed above my left breast?"

I was going for the former when I printed out the Wyoming state symbol on a plain piece of printer paper and got in my Jeep headed for Brattleboro, Vermont. My fraternity brother's parents were throwing a graduation party for him, and I found a nice little tattoo shop just a few miles from the town center that told me it was first come, first serve. I was twenty-two and clueless: *Of course* I can attend my friend's party and get a tattoo on the same day. The world is my oyster!

I made sure when I arrived in Vermont to hit the party first. I walked by a bunch of nice adults I had never met before and went straight up to the honoree, Chris.

"Colbert, you made it!" he exclaimed with excitement and surprise. For the past year I had become a little bit of a wild card. Once I got over the depressing part of grieving, I blossomed into kind of a party animal. I was on Prozac, loving life, and I said yes to everything. I wasn't doing drugs or blacking out, but I had self-centered social ADD, so naturally some people like Chris didn't always expect me to show up to something unless it benefited me.

"Damn right I did!" I said, like the broey college grad that I was. "Now here is your gift. I gotta run to my appointment at the tattoo parlor. Then I'll be back!"

Chris laughed, thinking I was joking. My creepy smile confirmed I was not.

"Wait, really?" he said, a little bummed but too nice to say it.

"Yeah, don't worry, it'll be quick. This thing goes till, like, seven, right?[2] Also, don't open this in front of your parents." I leaned in and said in a heavy whisper, "It's full of condoms."

He burst out into laughter, which I took as my cue to exit. I slapped his shoulder, put my perfectly cleaned Oakleys on, and headed back out the way I came: toward my car, full of narcissism.

. . .

---

2. This is extremely cringy for me to reflect upon as a grown man now.

"What's up?" I said as I entered the tattoo parlor.

The guy behind the counter wasn't threatening or anything, even though he had enough tats to make me think otherwise. Had he been to prison before? Likely not. He probably just got bored working at a tattoo shop in the middle of Vermont. I imagine it's like working at a hair salon, except less gossipy.

I, on the other hand, looked like the opposite of someone who had gone to prison. Polo and khaki shorts. Okay, maybe a prison for white-collar crimes. Anyway, this wardrobe is great for a dressy function, but not for a tattoo appointment. "I called earlier. I'd like to get this tattooed on my ankle," I said as I handed him the printout of the little bucking bronco.

He looked it over, probably disappointed that it wasn't a tramp stamp or because, in hindsight, it's the most boring tattoo of all time visually.

"That's fine. Take a seat. We'll call you when we're ready."

I nodded, then took a seat, thinking this would be quick.

It wasn't.

Two hours later, a tattoo artist we'll call Steve came from the back over to me. He was holding my printout. "Is this what you want as a tattoo?" he asked.

"Yeah, it's in honor of my dad who passed–"

He cut me off. "Cool. Yeah, so this won't work this small."

I leaned in closer as he pointed to the logo. It was about an inch or so high. Nice and subtle for one's first tattoo. Guaranteed to soften the blow of shock, too, when it was presented to outspoken family members. Which basically meant everyone in my family.

He continued. "At this size it's impossible to get the detail. His hand will be attached to his head; the horse will look like a blob. I can't get that detailed."

I've seen so many tattoos to this day that look like Da Vinci carved them. Tattoo artists can do amazing things with those tiny needles. So either Steve was garbage at his craft or he was right. Either way this was a wrench in the mix for sure. I had driven over two hours to get this tattoo. Oh, and yeah, to attend my buddies graduation party.

I looked at the Wyoming logo again, trying to imagine this massive cowboy tattooed on my ankle for life. I could see my mom's book club gossiping about my downfall. "Such a handsome, unmarked boy. And then his father passed away..."

I looked up at Steve. I felt lame being surrounded by people waiting to get things like a boa constrictor tattooed across their neck, but I couldn't help but nervously say something. I mean, this shit was for life.

"Hm. I'm worried about it being too big. Y'know?"

He looked at me, then at the image. "Let me show you what I'm thinking." He then went back to his office, most likely to make fun of me or do a shot of Jager. Maybe even both. I made eye contact with a girl across from me. Something about a woman actually not minding or better yet *wanting* the pain of a tattoo piqued a weird, bad girl alert in my downstairs area. I gave her a flirtatious smile to see if she felt the same. She quickly looked around for anything to grab to pretend she was busy and settled on *Rolling Stone* magazine.

I should go home.

· · ·

Before I knew it, I was sitting in Steve's tattoo bay with the new printout in hand. The logo I had printed off the internet eight hours prior had grown from a safe size to "Sweet mother of god, John got a tattoo!" While I was hesitant at first, I finally just said fuck it. I don't know if was trying to impress the girl in the lobby or piss off my mom's book club.[3] Either way I needed to get this tattoo because my father couldn't. Plus, this is why Macy's invented high-cut socks for men.

While Steve was getting his tools ready, Lobby Girl was escorted into the bay across the hall from mine. I got excited because as she lay back on the recliner she was still in plain view of me. Was I being creepy? Obviously. I then watched as she pulled her shirt up, exposing her belly.

"Is she getting a tattoo on her stomach?" I asked my new bestie Steve.

He leaned over to see what I was looking at. "Oh yeah. She's hardcore. I think she's in the Marines or some shit. The stomach is no joke."

"How so?"

"Hurts like fucking hell," he replied. I then watched as Lobby Girl made a face like she was bored as her guy began to tattoo her belly. She just lay there motionless, except for a few winces throughout, like she was on the toilet and generally relaxed.

I gulped like I was in a cartoon. "How bad is mine gonna hurt?"

I didn't mean to sound like a wimp, and yes, I didn't care about the pain since my tattoo had a higher meaning than most. Sorry, but it's a tad more special than a tattoo of Goofy on someone's butt cheek because they love Epcot!

Steve smirked. "It'll be a stinging pain every time the needle touches down. Not bad, though."

"Sounds kinda bad to me," I joked.

Steve laughed, then proceeded to brand my ankle with a cowboy on a bucking bronco. He was right. It only hurt every time the needle touched my skin. Unfortunately the needle touched my skin about 500 times. Every time he had to readjust or take a two-second break or even just to sit back to make sure he was copying the printout well, it was like a stinging sensation. Probably a five on the pain scale. Meanwhile, Lobby Girl was across the hall getting what probably felt like a cattle prod driven into her belly over and over. I think I even heard her burp at one point. Was she eating in there? I'm still into it.

A half hour later Steve was done with me and the basic-ass tattoo I had requested. No intricate details. Just a solid, colored-in shape. Real cool, John. That's how twenty-two-year-old me rolled. Steve put petroleum jelly on it, then wrapped my ankle in Saran Wrap.

"Keep this on it all day. Then any time you go in the sun for the next few months, put sunblock on it. Otherwise it'll fade."

I thanked him, said something like, "Wow, looks awesome," and then shook his hand. I was honestly really happy with it. And it was a rush getting a tattoo. You feel like you're doing something daring, illegal, and scary, yet you can't go to jail for it. Talk about ideal. It was my first one, and I was already ready for my second. I looked down at my new right ankle with pride. I knew my father would have loved it. That's all that mattered.

By the time I was done it was about six p.m. I didn't bother going to my buddy's party after all. I was sadly exhausted from sitting all day in a tattoo parlor, and I was ready to drive back to Massachusetts. Plus, my girlfriend at the time was excited to see it. Her house was on the drive home, and she said she was picking up Wendy's. Again, I was twenty-two.

I should've called Chris and told him I had a two-hour drive ahead of me and was exhausted. Instead I took the easy way out and texted him:

Hey, buddy. Finally just left tattoo parlor. It looks sick! Hope the party was fun. I gotta drive home now. Enjoy those condoms! Don't just use them for masturbating!!

Shame, party of one.

I'm happy I got the tattoo. Even if every time someone sees it they can't tell what it is. Or if my ankle is exposed at work from my jeans people are always shocked.

"You have a tattoo?!" they exclaim.

I nod, knowing I'm going to have to tell them the elevator pitch behind its meaning. Everyone loves the story, though; it's the actual tattoo that's another story. Like my wife's grandmother Flo the first time she saw it. Flo is a sweetheart with a good amount of Irish in her, just minus the accent.

"What is that supposed to be, honey?" she asked.

"A bucking bronco," I explained. "It's the Wyoming state symbol. My dad and I were gonna get it as tattoos when we went there on a family trip. We ran out of time, so when he passed away, I vowed to get it for him."

She leaned in, with me hopping on one leg so she could try to see my ankle at eye level.

"I still don't see it, love, but that's a really nice story."

Case in point.

STAGE 3: COMPLAINING IS THE NAME OF THE GAME

Time to be insufferable, you've earned it.

CHAPTER 7
SELF-CENTERED, FULL THROTTLE

HAVE you ever done something awful that only benefited you? Have you ever put someone else's needs or interests aside in favor of your own? Have you ever made an elderly neighbor cry?

If you answered yes to any of these, then you are ready to grieve!

When you deal with something heavy like death, and the smoke finally clears, you start showering on a daily basis, and doing that thing called smiling—you enter your SAF phase.

Selfish as fuck.

The SAF phase happens because you were dealt a really lousy hand and feel like it isn't fair that no one else had to go through what you went through. Why doesn't the guy down the street who is mean to everyone have to deal with this? Why doesn't Michael Bolton have to drink gross health shakes in a hospital bed? Everyone, in your perception, seems to be unscathed and blessed while you were in your own version of 'Nam.

Does that mean you need to steamroll over everyone's feelings to benefit your own? Nope. But that's what it becomes. In your mind, no matter how bad their week is, yours trumps it. Did they watch their dad exhale his last few breaths while draped in a stupid, blue fleece blanket that Sarah's ex gave us? Oh, they didn't?! Aw, yeah, okay then, I have the upper hand! Armed with such feelings, you become a human Gatling gun, blazing a trail that leaves friends, family, and even complete strangers in the dust.

The morning of my dad's funeral, Pookie's friends from church stopped by to help since they knew we'd have a lot on our plates. Anything we needed, they were ready to assist.

Define 'anything.'

Mrs. Showstead and I stood there in the garage, staring at brown paper bags full of empty beer and soda cans that had to be returned.

"You would like me to take these to the grocery store so you can get the deposit?" Mrs. Showstead asked, clearly hoping that by saying it out loud I'd realize how stupid it was.

I doubled down. "Yeah... is that okay? I mean, you can take them to the dump... Whatever is easiest." This was my attempt at making the task seem 'not so bad.'

"Okay, yeah... I can do that," she replied as she swallowed her dignity and kneeled to assess the damage.

"Great, thanks!" I said as I walked away. What the fuck did I just do? Did I ask a grown woman to help me with my chores? Well, yeah! There were so many chores lately with my dad gone that it was insane!

John, can you lift this?

John, can you change this light bulb?

John, can you replace Dad both emotionally and financially?

I was overwhelmed! So when a kind soul asked if they could help, I responded honestly. The second I walked away, though, I felt awful. Who was I? Was this who I had become? A twenty-year-old villain who treats sweet old ladies from church as the help? I felt like I couldn't just leave her working to go be lazy, so I pretended I was about to take on a project myself to justify me not returning the empties.

"Looks like this doorway could use some WD-40," I said loudly enough for Mrs. Showstead to hear me. The jingling of the bottles was becoming louder as she struggled to transport them into a bag that wouldn't burst open the second she lifted it off the ground. It's like she had never done this before. I added one more line to fill the awkward silence.

"Think we have some in the kitchen. Be right back!"

But I wasn't right back. Instead I retreated to the kitchen, took a deep breath, and then slowly made my way to the screened-in porch over the garage. I heard the clink of a can as it hit the driveway. I crept closer to the window to peer over and see the commotion. Mrs. Showstead was loading the brown bags into the trunk of her car. She was struggling with one, resting it on her hip so she could free a hand to open the trunk. I stood there watching it all from a safe distance, frozen with social awkwardness. *What does one do in this situation?* I wondered. *I could offer to drive. Offer to take over.* I looked around. *She could help tidy up in the kitchen instead. Or fold laundry. Or just sit with my mom and listen.*

I got closer to the screen window. I had to do something.

"Mrs. Showstead!"

She turned all around, trying to find the source of the yell. She was struggling.

"Up here."

She found me.

"Yes?"

"Try Roche Brothers in Wellesley. They have the machine out front for the cans."

She politely smiled, growing blind from the sun beaming directly into her face.

"Oh, and thank you! Can't say that enough! Or should I say CAN'T say that enough!" I then laughed at my own joke.

She nodded at the pun, then got into her car. As she pulled out of the driveway I waved goodbye, but she couldn't see me. There were bags of cans piled so high in the back they blocked her rearview mirror.

My dad was just getting settled into heaven that day while I was clearly headed for hell.

I think it's worth noting that no one properly prepared me for what happens after you lose a loved one. Every self-help book on the subject is serious, formal, and doesn't point out any of the perks. Yes, there are perks to losing a loved one besides the helpful church ladies.

There's the free meals.

I'm not talking like a greasy pizza or some cold cuts for sandwiches. I'm talking huge casserole dishes filled to the brim with warm lasagna, accompanied by a salad and rolls and dropped off by some super-nice neighbor to your front door.

Daily.

You're probably thinking to yourself, "Yikes, did John never get home-cooked meals growing up?" Calm down, Karen, we did. We got all the standards: chicken with a side of peas, spaghetti and meatballs, and the half-ass classic that I secretly love and make almost nightly for my kids now—plain pasta with salt and butter. Don't judge, just try it. Pookie cooked just about every night while holding down a full-time job, but once my dad started living at the hospital, none of us had the energy to properly cook. We'd pick up random meals at the grocery store or we'd pick up a pizza and get even more fat.

So to suddenly have the doorbell ring and you now have something to actually cheer you up, like warm food? You felt pampered even if it was just one meal a day. Honestly we ate better during my dad's death and bereavement than we did growing up. And we belonged to a country club.

I guess that means I should've known better as far as etiquette and manners, but the SAF phase takes no prisoners.

It was the week that was designated for my mom's book club to bring us dinner, and it was during one of these book club dinner drop-offs that this particularly awful example presented itself.

The victim? We'll call her Lisa, not only to protect her but also because at the time she was a MILF and I don't want her reading this and feeling super awkward about it. Also I can't remember her name, and if I call Pookie right now, she's not going to give me the correct answer. Instead she'll vent to me about whatever piece of her house is falling apart this week.

The point is, "Lisa" was attractive, not to mention very kind for bringing us a home-cooked meal. Unfortunately for her, I was home when she did. The doorbell echoed throughout our modestly large house. I wish I could say I was busy consoling my mother, who had just lost her husband of, like, thirty-two years or that I was going through what of his possessions could be donated to small children in Uganda. Instead I was watching *Happy Gilmore* for the fourth time that week and periodically checking my pits to make sure I still could hold off from showering.

When I heard the doorbell, I proceeded to gracefully swing the door open like that was going to be her big turn-on. There Lisa stood, five-foot-five with dirty blonde hair and a face too gorgeous to be hidden in the suburbs. We could have had a fun summer together: both at our sexual peaks, both conveniently living on the same street. Imagine the fling! Had she ever been with a gangly ginger before? Sure, I'd most likely disappoint her in and out of the bedroom, but she didn't know that yet. If I played things cool maybe, just maybe, this could lead to us hanging out.

"Oh! I didn't know you were home. Thought it was just Natalie and your mom," she said.

I played the whole thing aloof. Super chill, super stupid.

"I'm home from college until, like... the end of the week. Maybe I'll go back if there are any wicked good parties, we'll see" I said.

She looked down at her casserole dish in a panic.

"I wish I had known... I only made enough for the two of them. Maybe I should've made more," she said, eager to please.

"Yeah, there's a bunch of us. My sisters might even come by," I said, being sarcastic.

She stood there speechless for a second, like she was holding back tears.

She mumbled a quiet "okay" then headed back to her car, still holding the dish.

Did I stop her and apologize? I wish.

Which is why two hours later, when she came back with not one, but two casserole dishes, I pretended to be busy and made Pookie answer the door instead. Pookie waited until the door was fully closed and Lisa was in her car before commenting.

"Lisa just dropped off two dishes and said, 'Sorry, hope this is enough for everyone.' Why the heck did she make so much food?!"

"Beats me! She's weird," I yelled.

"I'll say," Pookie said.

"Oh no," I said on the phone. I was standing in my cubicle at my first advertising job. It was 2005 in New York City—two years after my father's death and the SAF phase was wearing thin.

"Poor guy," I said. Then I listened to Sami explain to me that my grandpa Jack, my dad's dad, had passed away. He had been in rougher shape over the past two years. He had been moved into assisted living, where my Uncle Fred visited him often. I think they had even found prostate cancer.

"So the service is this weekend," Sami was saying.

"Ooh. Hm."

"Yuuppppp," Sami added.

The last of your dad's parents just died. The service is this weekend. Take the train or bus home to Boston from New York. Easy.

Ehhh, not so much. That was Labor Day weekend. And my sister and I? We were assholes.

"Leah invited us to their Cape house. I mean, it's a big holiday weekend. I don't know why they'd do it this weekend."

I could sense the fear in Sami's voice. She was really looking forward to these plans. Plus a small percentage of her had a fair point—people could have already been out of town and might miss the service. Mostly, though, she just wanted to be at the beach and not a funeral home.

I was beginning to think she had the right idea.

"Greg did say we could go to his shore house this weekend."

There it was. I was beginning to turn in a direction that benefitted only me. We hung up in agreement that our beach weekends away were more important than showing up to one of the four funerals you're alloted for your biological grandparents. I acted like there was one to attend every year. No one was forcing us to go. At least not directly. Me being five hours away in Manhattan didn't help. Like going to Mom when you know Dad will say no, I confided in a co-worker I knew would have my back.

"It's my grandfather's funeral this weekend. I should take off Friday so I can make it, but my buddy also invited me to his beach house down the shore."

Mirra looked around to make sure the coast was clear, which it was, then looked me dead in the eyes. She was attractive with incredible eye contact, so I got both relaxed and nervous at the same time. (It can happen.) She gave me the game plan, as if we were going to stage my own death.

"Tell your boss you had a death in the family. You need to

take off Friday to attend the service, and you'll be back Monday."

"Should I say I'll be on email or I can call in as needed?" I asked.

She shook her head. "You said all you needed to say, and they can't question you on that."

Damn, she was good.

So was the Jersey Shore. I mean, it was Labor Day weekend. Fuhgeddaboudit! I boogie-boarded, I grilled, I went out to bars. You know what I didn't do? Realize that it wasn't about being at the funeral for my grandfather, per se. The dude was dead. He'd have no idea if I made an appearance or not. It was about being there for my family. For my cousins as our family continued to get taken down by so many loved ones passing. It also could have helped me, as I was still in the heavy throws of my grieving journey.

Even better, I could've been there for my uncle Fred, who lost his brother two years back, and now had lost his father. I would've been the only man there who knew the emotional journey that he had just begun and could never reverse the effects of: losing a father as a son.

CHAPTER 8
PEAS AND THANK YOU

"SOOOO," I said awkwardly.

"Soo," Pookie replied.

We chuckled as we stood in the office of the home that I had grown up in. I had just driven from Keene State for the first Thanksgiving break without my father. My car was still full of my crap out in the driveway. I had come in to pee before unloading when I heard papers ruffling. I found Pookie standing over the pool table, which was in the center of the room. Every square inch of felt was covered by bills and various magazines and paperwork. This is what happens when the job of two people falls on one. Who happens to hoard.

I stared at a bill that Pookie was rereading. She read the first page, then the second, and repeated this process over and over until I interrupted in an effort to solidify our plans for the next day.

"Wait, sorry. What are we doing tomorrow?" I asked.

"We're driving to Ellen's. She invited us."

"What are Sami and Sarah doing?" I asked.

"I think Sami is going to Todd's parents' in New Hampshire. Sarah is going to Dave's parents' house for the day."

Natalie entered the room.

"What do you wanna do?" Pookie asked me.

"Eat and sleep," I joked, but not really.

Pookie nodded in agreement. Aunt Ellen, her sister-in-law, was a good cook. All we'd have to do was drive an hour to Nashua, and we'd be served the works. Even so, neither one of us felt like even lifting a set of keys to put into the ignition. Suddenly all I wanted to do was be hand-fed mint Milanos while I lay on the leather couch like a baroque painting.

"Do we have food here if we don't go to Ellen's?" I asked.

"I have a leftover quiche."

"From when Dad was first diagnosed?"

She raised her eyebrow and gave me such a quick glare it knocked the wind out of me. Despite our sluggish and introverted vibes, we had to go somewhere for Thanksgiving. If we didn't, we'd feel even more depressed, or worse.

Starved.

On Thanksgiving Day, I pulled Pookie's "Nantucket red" Volvo V70 wagon into Aunt Ellen's and Uncle Larry's driveway. Pookie rode shotgun and Natalie took the back seat. She made a joke at Grandpa Joe's expense.

"Hope Grandpa didn't overdress today in a suit!" Natalie quipped, then quickly backpedaled. "Oh, just kidding; never mind."

The previous summer, when my uncle went to pick up Grandpa Joe, my mom's dad, for a casual barbecue, he was dressed to the nines in his finest corduroy three-piece suit. It was July in New England, meaning ninety-five degrees out at ninety-five percent humidity. My uncle quickly made him change, and the story spread like wildfire. Poor guy. He was starting to experience a little dementia, and as you've learned, we're a tough crowd. Unlike Grandpa Joe, we never forget.

Ten minutes later we were all sitting around Uncle Larry and Aunt Ellen's nice living room, having our glasses of wine before turkey dinner, when the topic of my life after college graduation in the spring came up. Someone asked what I'd like to do, and I gave my usual answer of 'write and direct movies.' This time I added more. "I'd like to move to LA. That's just where most of the industry is."

"That would be fun. Larry and I went to California years ago," Aunt Ellen chimed in, clearly a fan of this plan.

My other uncle, Jay, leaned in quietly and intensely. "You know I know the editor at *Variety*."

"Wow, that's cool," I replied, all chipper. I could use any connection I could get. Unfortunately, most led to empty promises. A year later, when I was struggling in LA to find work, I'd take him up on that connection. He'd never return my call. My uncle Jay is a unique individual. He lived in France for a while, where he 'ran a performing arts center.' I put that in air quotes because whenever I've seen him since, he has wild stories about racing Ferrari's in India and avoiding being raped or killed in South Africa. Either his performing arts center is funded by blood diamonds, he's in the CIA, or he's just fucking with me. I'm going with option C. Eventually he moved back to the states with his new partner, Marie Paul, a very nice opera singer he met in France. She has a French accent, loves wine, and is very pleasant to converse with. What's not to like?

After my 'cool!' reply, Jay leaned back in his chair. He seemed satisfied with my enthusiasm towards his *Variety* connection as the conversation sputtered along.

"Now, will you drive cross-country with your son, Cheryl?" Uncle Larry joked.

Larry, my mom's other brother, has been making dad jokes since before social media made them popular. He's extremely nice and well-traveled. His mother, my grandmother Phyllis, would say he's 'sensitive,' as if that's a negative. But she smoked like a chimney, so I'll take 'sensitive' over 'smokey' any day.

Speaking of which, Grandma Phyllis was sitting on the same couch as Grandpa Joe. The two had divorced ten years prior but still came to some of the same events.

"Maybe you could get a job sooner and save up for Los Angeles," Grandma Phyllis said. She came from a very hard-working generation. A kid moving to a glamorous city to pursue their passion sadly wasn't a concept she was used to.

When it comes to your passionate job interest or search, most people will say something supportive and move on.

Family has a different approach, one that is one part unsolicited advice, and two parts nothing they would ever consider themselves if the shoe was on the other foot.

"Have you considered the hitman trade?" Grandpa Joe asked.

Not only did I lose my dad eight months ago, but my new guidance counselor has dementia. *This should end well,* I thought.

"Seriously?" I asked.

He smiled as he nodded. He seemed almost excited. Like he had been waiting until I was the proper age to suggest this. Suddenly the conversation shifted.

"Cheryl, did you hear that Becky and Carl are getting divorced?" My Aunt Ellen is like one of those toys for kids that has six octopus arms; you hook a hose up to it and plop it on the lawn when it's ninety degrees out. When you're a kid, half the fun is never knowing where it's gonna spray next. Less so with Aunt Ellen, but she had clearly moved on from the Los Angeles conversation.

"Becky from nursing school?" my mom responded.

But Grandpa Joe hadn't moved on.

"Think about it," he told me.

"The hitman thing?" I responded.

"Yes."

We now had two conversations going. Could we get a third?

"Danielle, are you going to live with Pookie again this summer?" Natalie joked.

The answer was yes, yes, we could.

"Ah, wine," I said and began to chug. My cousin Danielle noticed, and we both cracked up as she began to respond to Natalie. That's when I turned back to Grandpa Joe. This was like responding to a telemarketer when you have no desire to buy what they're selling but you have nothing better to do. I was grieving, and we came in one car.

"Who says I'm cut out to kill people for a living?" I said with a slight grin. Danielle and I exchanged another look, and she nearly lost it.

"Now I know you don't believe me," he said, "but seriously

it's not a bad idea. There's good money in it. Someone always needs to be taken out."

"You want me to kill people for money? How would I even get into that?"

He replied, deadpan, "I know some people."

Was he onto something? Probably. Would I be loaded? Yes. Would I take to it quickly because it's a form of freelance and that's my favorite way to operate? Yes. Would I also be dead in prison by now if I had? Also yes.

If you're wondering how my mother felt about her father giving her son illegal career advice, she had moved on.

"Was it drugs?" Pookie asked Ellen with a strong touch of shade to her question. That seemed to not be a factor Ellen had considered as they gossiped about god knows who.

After that murder-for-hire chat, I felt surprisingly famished. Natalie went up to our mom and mumbled something in such a whiny tone it sounded like a cat dying.

"I'M SORRY, WHAT?!" my mom screamed even though Natalie was a foot away.

"I said *I'm hungry*. Are we going to eat soon?"

I piped in. Felt like I had to. "Jesus, you two, keep it down." They were embarrassing. I did my usual nervous trait of laughing it off as Larry came by.

"Let's get our drinks and make our way to the dining room!" he said.

Perfect timing. A few more minutes and I think Natalie was going to gnaw a chunk out of the walnut coffee table.

We were settling in at the dining room table, about to dive into the beautiful spread Ellen had slaved over, when Larry realized only one thing was missing besides my father.

"I think we forgot the peas! Ellen, should I grab them?"

"No, they aren't ready yet."

"They were ready a moment ago. What changed?"

"Larry, not now!" Ellen barked, then stormed out of the room.

Larry turned to us to save face. "You all may eat. We'll bring them out when they're ready for the second time," he said, then chuckled at his own joke.

Pookie, unable to read the room, said, "I love peas. Hopefully they're ready soon."

I looked down and shook my head. Someone raised their glass to make a toast.

"Is Ellen coming back? Let's wait for her," Jay said.

"Ellen, dear, do you want help?!" Larry yelled towards the kitchen.

There wasn't a peep from the kitchen.

Tension was filling the air, and my gravy was beginning to cool down. Larry, sensing trouble, excused himself from the table just before giving us all a courteous smile, like a manager who is going to go back to the kitchen to find a line cook on fire.

Murmurs and bickering emitted ever so gently from the kitchen.

I took a bite out of a roll, trying not to make a sound. Someone else forked a piece of turkey while trying to not scrape their plate. If we were going to eavesdrop, we had to be silent. Unfortunately it was impossible to make out what they were saying.

I attempted to break the silence with a subtle joke. "Honestly I'm not even that big on peas."

"Maybe she's just reheating them," Pookie said.

"Oh my god, Mom, since when do you like peas so much?!"
I snapped.

Danielle and Natalie chuckled.

Suddenly there was a loud bang in the other room. A nice piece of China slammed itself onto the kitchen floor.

"GOD DAMN IT!" Ellen screamed.

The peas were down. I repeat, the peas were down.

We froze.

"It's okay, let's just scoop them back in the bowl," Larry said quietly.

But Ellen had thrown in the towel. "BUT THEY WERE ON THE FLOOR, LARRY!"

I smiled and tried not to laugh. I felt bad, but also this just felt on theme for how the year had gone up until this moment. First a funeral, now the peas. *How much more could we lose?!* I was halfway through stuffing my face to cope with the awkwardness when our hosts returned. With the bowl of peas. They were glowing with greenness as the steam wafted off the bowl like it was in a food commercial. If the entire table was full or hated peas, you wouldn't have known it.

"Yum, those look great!" Grandpa Joe suddenly stood up to help grab the bowl and feed himself. I've never seen him move so quickly. He took a heaping scoop, way more than he could physically eat, and passed it to Phyllis.

"Did you make these from scratch? They look fresh!" Pookie chimed in, being way too obvious.

One by one we all excitedly helped ourselves to the peas that may or may not have spent some time on the kitchen floor.

If the peas had caused a scene, Phyllis's fresh blueberry pie saved the day. Honestly it's what I miss most about her. The woman made amazing pies.

That evening me and "The Golden Girls," Natalie and Pookie, returned to our big, quiet house. We stepped through the front door, and like three cars that each took a different exit, we spread out to find our own sense of reprieve. "I'm exhausted," Pookie said, but as her business phone rang in the office, she quickly ran to answer it and was chatting away to someone who was most likely her business partner, Fran, on the other end.

Natalie went up to her bedroom to "change into her jammies," and I headed to the fridge for some flat seltzer someone hadn't closed tightly enough. I headed to the basement to see if there might be any new bottles still around.

All I found in the basement was a jug of Tide from Costco the size of a Buick. But I found myself wandering down the basement hallway to the old racquetball court. It had been a while since I'd been in there. It was a cement cube about six hundred square feet that you stepped down a few stairs into. There were old, protective cages over the lights, and the ceiling of the racquetball court was about twenty feet high. The previous owner used it to hit golf balls into a mat. We used it mostly for street hockey and ping-pong.

On winter school nights, my father would bug me to play ping-pong with him. He'd dip his head in my room as I was doing my geometry homework.

"Care for a game?" he'd ask, giddy.

"I have so much homework to do."

"Just one game."

We'd smile, both knowing we were about to play.

It was always 'first to twenty-one,' and he never would cap it at just one game. It was always two to three games, and no matter if I walked away after the first or the fifth, he always begged for one more.

As I flicked the lights on and stood there, there was a coldness around me. Not just weather-wise, seeing as in New England the Thanksgiving temps were fifteen degrees on a good day, but with an oddness now that was becoming the new normal. Fewer people, even just one less, made for a quieter atmosphere. Today was odd. Not because my grandfather's career advice included homicide or because of the fallen peas, but because I had learned that the holidays would never be the same ever again.

The location, vibe, and people will change. It will get better. But one person will always be marked absent. I can't tell you how much the reality of that sinking in took my breath away. Even the racquetball room—which was full of hockey sticks, a ping-pong table, and random sports gear we'd use to make this room louder than a KISS concert on nights like this when we'd all come down after a holiday meal—felt suddenly stale and dead. Like an abandoned amusement park that used to be so full of life, now it was so quiet you could hear the wind over the rides.

It was enough to make me cry a little. I wiped the last rogue tear away, then found myself heading back upstairs to the kitchen to make microwave popcorn. Crying and eating are not mutually exclusive.

Maybe Christmas would be better.

CHAPTER 9
MERRY F*CKING CHRISTMAS

IT SHOULD BE no surprise that we didn't respond to a lot of holiday party invites that year. The mixture of muffled tears and short tempers really ruins any Bing Crosby song no matter how much you turn it up. We felt like we should spare people. So when Christmas Eve arrived, we had no solid plans besides possibly going to one of the evening holiday services at church and a possible visit to Uncle Fred's the next day. If my dad was around, none of these would have been a 'possibly.' They'd all be locked in.

Thanksgiving, while odd, was a good warm-up. The holidays are the hardest part after someone is gone. A time that is supposed to be full of joy and cheer and family now feels daunting and broken. The support you got eight months ago has fully fizzled out by now. You're no longer the biggest dumpster fire in everyone's social circle. If you reach out, you get good responses, but no one checks in as much as they used to. You feel like a loner compared to your peers. Not to mention your cousins who still have both their parents. I'd eventually gain something truly superhuman and beneficial from this whole experience but at the time, it was hard to see the silver linings.

The biggest invisible silver lining being that my dad wasn't in an ICU undergoing chemo. Not worrying about his discomfort spending the holidays in a sterile hospital was a big relief. Or when he did come home for a bit of time and I'd see his sisters laugh in front of him, then cry in the privacy of the hallway. The show was over. While it was miserable, it was still a form of stimulation. Without it and the people that came with it, which was a social factor, one can start to feel lethargic and hopeless. Every week it increased by such a small amount it was hard to see at the time.

Hindsight is 20/20.

Since we commuted for Thanksgiving, we wanted to stay home for Christmas. Or at least Christmas Eve. In addition to me, Pookie, and Natalie, Sarah was joining us, which was nice. I was excited to have more of the immediate family around compared to the last holiday. We'd also be getting a grandparent for a sleepover.

My mother's mother, Grandma Phyllis, was coming to spend the night so she could be with us Christmas morning. She had done this just about every year, but this year was different. This year the need for visitors was higher. As was the need for comfort food, and as I've mentioned, Phyllis made incredible pies. Specifically blueberry pie with fresh whipped cream. While I wasn't ready to help host a visitor, I was looking forward to what possible signs of warmth this woman could bring to an otherwise cold house as of late. She was not an affectionate woman, but if she could bring dessert, help around the house, and maybe get us all to play one of her card games like Kings in the Corner, it could just be the support we needed during a truly difficult time.

Every year, per tradition, she'd let herself in, and upon no one greeting her in the foyer, because we were usually running around at the last minute, getting ready to host, she'd impatiently yell, "Well? I'm here!" Someone would rush over apologizing as they took her coat. My dad without fail would sarcastically say under his breath as he passed me on the stairwell, "Oh, good. Phyllis is here."

You don't learn this until you get older. Like over-forty older. But those are the 'traditions' you miss when someone is gone. They're annoying at the time, but later you learn to appreciate them and worse—long for them. Years later Grandma Phyllis passed away, and I found myself missing her flaws. Her armless hugs, her Parliament Lights, and her annual Christmas Eve arrival.

Now that my father was gone I found myself taking on his role as she pulled into the driveway.

"Oh good, Phyllis is here," I said as I looked out the second-floor hallway window.

"Shit," said Pookie as she rushed to her room still in her bathrobe.

Phyllis was soon indoors and posted up in the kitchen with a fresh cup of herbal tea. The woman drank five cups a day of the stuff. On about her third cup Sarah walked in with an overflowing mountain of laundry. "Well, I'm here!" she said, doing her best Grandma Phyllis impression. Grandma was amused and didn't realize the imitation was of her. Sarah was giving

Phyllis a real hug but not getting the same in return when some of the roommates got testy.

"No, I'll do it later!" Natalie belted out as she put her dirty cereal bowl in the sink, defiant toward my mother who was standing nearby, still in her robe.

"Natalie, it's important to do as your mother said," Phyllis commented. Her true words were wasted on the youth. Natalie was already shaking her head and beginning to drift toward the far side of the room, just within earshot in case the convo got good and she needed to creep back in.

I felt the need to address the larger issue at hand. "I'll say it right now: I don't know if I wanna go to church tonight, regardless of what time."

Every Christmas Eve the Wellesley Congregational Church did a few evening services in honor of the holiday. It was special and only for Christmastime. There was a six, eight, and ten p.m., and even a midnight service. Wild, I know.

"What if we do the earlier one? There's a six p.m., eight thirty, ten o'clock," Pookie replied.

Why do I even bother?

Sarah laughed. "Brad Sicchitano and his girlfriend might go to the ten p.m. one, actually."

"Cow Tongue?" I asked. Brad and Sarah had dated for a little while back in high school, and apparently when they made out, she said it was like making out with a cow. Not sure how she found that metaphor. Regardless, I liked Brad. Nice, funny guy. But not even Brad could get me psyched about church, let alone at night.

"*Ugh...*" I let out a groan with no shame. Without my father around, I found myself more outspoken. At the moment I was not only outspoken. I was also outnumbered.

"The choir is supposed to sing at the ten o'clock service. That could be fun!" Natalie said.

God damn it. The kid was twelve. Now we *had* to go. Plus I think Pookie must've napped because she seemed wired.

Phyllis planted a seed to get herself out of church, and possibly out of Christmas in general if she wanted. "There might be a bad storm tomorrow."

All of us swiveled our heads toward her. Here the fuck we go.

"How much?" I asked.

"I heard on the drive up here more than a few inches. What worries me is if the roads are icy."

Sarah and I exchanged a look. This wasn't the first time Phyllis had gotten anxious about potential weather. Last Christmas morning (weeks before doctors found my dad's tumors), Grandma woke us up at eight a.m. to quickly blow through all the presents so she could get on the road and head home before the storm got worse. We then sat there with bad breath and nothing to do until our dinner guests arrived eight hours later... as a mere inch of snow fell outside.

"Now what?!" my father had barked. It was the latest in a long track record of this behavior, hence the sarcastic tone he had when she would arrive every year.

I vowed to never let that happen again.

"When is it supposed to start? You could stay an extra day or leave tonight?"

Everyone laughed. I wasn't kidding. I preferred the former. I mean, my dad died, and it would have been nice to have one of my only living grandparents stick around for a bit. Another warm body in the house. Not asking for a lot here.

"What's the plan for tomorrow?" Sarah asked. "We could go for a walk. Make a yummy breakfast." We had a guest, and it suddenly gave us inspiration to make the best of things.

"I believe the storm starts tomorrow," Phyllis replied. "I just don't want the roads to be icy."

In case we didn't hear Scrooge the first two times.

"Well, let's watch the news later and see if there's an update," Pookie suggested. "In the meantime, the ten p.m. service?"

Nine forty-five rolled around and Phyllis was ready to hit the town.

"Well, looks like I'm the only one ready!" Phyllis barked. She was standing in her Sunday best judging the shit out of us. We've had a year, Phyllis! Technically we were ready, but our outfits were more fitting for a trip to K-Mart for a bucket of cheese balls. The Wellesley Congregational Church was nothing fancy, but you couldn't wear a bathrobe. Plus you never knew who you were gonna see. Grieving or not, I was newly single and ready to Christian mingle.

We made our way to the church, and the place was bumpin'. Pookie is more famous than J.Lo there. Everyone knew her and she had to talk to every single one of them. We were trying to pile into the pew an usher had kindly directed us to when Chatty Kathy was suddenly stopped dead in her tracks.

"Cheryl?" Phyllis asked.

Pookie was trying to mouth a conversation with her business partner, Fran, who was way across the other side of the room. Both suddenly were laughing at a joke. Either they had telepathy or dementia.

"Mom, will you move?" Sarah asked.

"Sarah, would you just stop!" Pookie snapped. She had awakened the beast. Church was *her* zone. Don't mess with it.

We eventually shuffled in, took our seats, and did that thing we all do when we sit on a wooden seat: we shimmied our asses side to side, thinking we could get comfy if we just flattened our butts the right way. I had found the right spot when all of a sudden someone turned around in the pew in front of us and flashed a grin.

"Hello, Colberts." It was Brad Sicchitano in the flesh.

"Heyyy," Sarah said, like some kind of Vegas lounge act.

Pookie, who moments ago had been ready to slap her middle daughter, turned on the charm. "How's your mother, Brad? Isn't this service lovely? This is my mother, Phyllis." They shook hands.

Brad was polite, upbeat, and happy. We soaked it up as he continued. "She's great actually. Oh, and I'd like you all to meet my girlfriend, Kelly." Kelly rotated around to say hi. I noticed two little girls seated next to her.

Brad asked the real important question: "How are you all holding up?"

We all responded at once.

"Barely!"

"Doing the best we can."

"Eh."

Sarah and I both laughed. As did Brad once he realized that was an option. It felt comforting seeing a familiar face. His radiant mood, probably because he wasn't grieving on Christmas Eve like us, helped give us all a little boost.

An hour later I unlocked the Volvo with the clicker, and we all piled in.

"She seems nice, Brad's girlfriend," Pookie said as she unfortunately took the front seat next to me. She never learned the rule that you can only back-seat drive from the back seats. Phyllis had called shotgun on the way here but somehow lost it for the drive home. Natalie was the last to get in. Once her door closed I started the engine. Pookie started hers as well.

"Is she older?" Pookie asked.

There it was.

"Kelly? Yes, I think so," Sarah responded briefly as to not fuel the fire.

I laughed, causing Pookie to retreat.

"Oh, she's super nice," she demurred. "I'm just asking. I'm not used to seeing a guy with an older woman is all."

"So she's a cougar?" Sarah made a meowing sound.

"Wait, what's that?" Pookie asked, amused. My mother is notorious for being overly curious about romance, sex, or anything else that would be inappropriate to ask your kids. When she started dating again about a year or so after my father's death, we all went out to dinner, including my siblings' husbands. The conversation naturally got dirty, and that's when Pookie chimed in.

"Has anyone ever... farted... during sex?"

She tried to backpedal off our disgusted looks.

"I've heard that can happen to people."

"Like you?!" Todd asked.

We all lost it.

Back in the Volvo on our way home, Sarah took the bait. "Yes, Mom, a cougar is an older woman dating a younger man. Usually wealthy, hot, et cetera."

I could feel the intrigue boiling in Pookie's brain. Recently forced to be single, she was wondering, *Can I be such a cougar?*

It was late when we got home. I suddenly didn't feel so great. Color was draining from my face and I was getting nauseous. I headed to my bathroom, shut the door, and proceeded to stand over the sink and try to throw up. Was this karma for us commenting on Brad's girlfriend? After a few dry heaves and some forced coughs to get things going, all I produced was a tiny bit of throw-up. It was bright green, because I had been chewing mint gum. Or because I was being festive?

"John... are you okay? Your mother thought she heard you throwing up," Phyllis kindly asked as I opened the door. She had a bad rap because she could be snappy, crabby, and other '-py' words. She wasn't a cold person, she just had poor bedside manner. Again, she made incredible pies. It balanced out.

"Well, hope you feel better, dear, for Christmas," Phyllis added.

"Thanks, Grandma." We're both horrible at giving affection, so we both smiled without showing our teeth, then swiveled around and headed toward our respective rooms for the evening. I wanted to tell her I was glad she was there. Even though I had just ralphed up some gum in the sink after talking to Cow Tongue at church, this first Christmas without Dad was already feeling a bit better than the first Thanksgiving. Her and Sarah being in the house was helping. Sarah made me laugh, and Grandma was a character that made me laugh as well, just not on purpose. I was thinking about how precious family is as I got into bed, exhausted and drained. Maybe after we opened gifts, we could make pancakes and bacon and all the fixings, then play cards by the fire. Grandma could also check out the blanket she had knit for us years ago that was comfy as hell but growing a huge hole. She brought her sewing stuff, right? Merry Christmas, Grandma... now fix this! I smirked at my own joke. Then my head hit the pillow, and I was out cold.

That's how it must've happened because the next morning I awoke to my bedside lamp still on and Sarah rocking a hideous old bathrobe from The Gap as she snooped around my room to see if my sleeping arrangements were better than hers. Middle child much?

"Can I help you?" I asked. My eyes felt glued shut.

"Merry Christmas!" Sarah said. "Now do you want the good news or bad news?"

"Oh god. Both."

"Old Phyllis wants us to open presents so she can get on the road before the storm comes."

"What's the good news?"

"There's freshly squeezed OJ," Sarah replied.

"Are you kidding me?!" I belted out. I felt exhausted, but not too tired to complain. She had had time to digest the news, so she wasn't as irate. I got out of bed and looked out the window. Phyllis was brushing off the pathetic amount of flurries that had fallen on her car. She looked like she had slept fully dressed, including her coat.

A half hour later, after the last present was opened, I could feel Phyllis trying to make eye contact with me. She wanted help; I could feel it. I tried to look every which way but up.

"Natalie, is that a Beanie Baby? Cool!" I grabbed the plush toy.

"Do you think–" Phyllis was bugging Pookie to get to me.

"Yup," Mom said, immediately on the same page. "Hey, John, do you think you could help Grandma?"

There was no point in fighting it. I looked up like I was ready to be executed.

Phyllis flashed me a warm smile. "Would you mind helping me get my suitcase from upstairs?"

"Sure," I muttered. I wanted to add, *Thanks for being so narcissistic today!*

With Phyllis fully loaded up and ready to go, I watched as she peeled out of the driveway at a rockin' 15 mph, leaving behind a grieving widow, two granddaughters, and a grandson. I closed the front door and found Sarah sprawled out on one end of the family room sofa with coffee. I crawled to the empty end to join her.

That's when the phone rang. I grabbed the remote and turned on the TV, knowing I likely would not turn it off until at least eight hours from now.

"It's Uncle Fred!" Pookie announced while covering the receiver. "He's checking to see if we wanna come over later. We don't have to bring anything, and they'd love to see us!" Fred was my dad's only brother, and every year we had alternated between hosting Christmas at our house or theirs. It was a big bash that usually concluded with a Yankee Swap and an incredible amount of dick jokes.

Sarah and I didn't take our eyes off *National Lampoon's Christmas Vacation.*

"Eh, not really," we both grunted. Grandma's drama had

drained us. Not to mention the whole year. At that moment, it felt like a train going 200 mph had suddenly slammed on its brakes and lost all steam. My body felt sluggish. It was more than just physical. I was mentally tired as well. I didn't know it at the moment, but the worst of this was yet to come.

The phone rang the second Pookie put it down, finishing her chat with Uncle Fred. She picked it up and after a moment her 'phone voice' quickly changed to normal.

Sarah turned to me. "Must be family."

"It's Grandma. She's home safe and wants to wish everyone a Merry Christmas!" Pookie yelled from the kitchen with enthusiasm.

Fuck you, Phyllis.

You know what the worst part is? I don't think she even brought pie.

CHAPTER 10
POPPIN' BOTTLES

CONTENT WARNING: *suicidal thoughts. Please read with care.*

The thrill of the "25 Days of Christmas" marathon on ABC Family was over, and I was feeling it. The stimuli of the spilled peas and the runaway grandmother had ended, and I had entered 'the grieving blues,' but I didn't realize it yet. Suddenly the need to set an alarm seemed very casual. A part-time holiday job fell through at the last minute, so what was the point? I had nothing but time and a secure internet connection.

Which was not a good thing.

For one thing, I found myself casually surfing for porn like I was window-shopping. "The lighting on this one looks good," I'd say to myself as I clicked through clips. Yes, these clips led to the inevitable matinee of masturbation plus a hint of guilt, but many times I circled back on certain sites throughout the day out of boredom. It was an addiction, like eating food for taste. My eyes were basically gaining weight.

Wait, did he just say he played with himself a lot?

Calm down. I wasn't going for the world record of masturbating. I was just a lazy twenty-year-old kid with way too much testosterone. That sex drive was very below the surface, for the rest of my brain and body had the energy levels of a cadaver. I was slowly slipping into a liminal place where time no longer mattered, and I couldn't muster up the ambition to work on anything besides voyeurism, be it a Chevy Chase movie or a porn parody of a Chevy Chase movie.

Elizabeth Kubler-Ross famously broke the grieving process down into five stages: denial, anger, bargaining, depression, and acceptance. Some smart people have broken it down into three, others twelve. These five make the most sense to me, as I remember all of them vividly. I remember yelling a lot at my ex before we broke up the fall after my father's death. I would go from discussion to yelling in 3.5 seconds, flat.

The first three weren't bad. And I've been in 'acceptance' for a while now. It's number four, depression, that was like a beautiful, friendly, rainbow-colored tree frog that you find out secretes a poison when it sneezes that'll give you night terrors while your skin eats itself. Underestimated danger. Depression was my tiny, venomous tree frog named... We'll name him Trevor for fun.

I didn't like what life had become eight months after my dad passed away. It was just Pookie, Natalie, and me at home. For the first time our large, charming house felt like a negative. Even a week earlier, with Phyllis arriving and us complaining about her, had been exciting compared to this. Rooms started to grow lonely. Was this how things were always going to be? I had been grieving over the loss of my father all year and didn't want to grieve any longer. I didn't want to feel any more pain. I just wanted to lie down and not have to worry ever again. This new feeling rolled in low and slow like a tsunami—and hit me just as hard—right as I was getting back to school for the second semester of my senior year.

Trevor transformed me. He created a new world in my mind that had no hope. Most people in my life don't know how far Trevor took me, but it went so far that I had one toe dipped in the "Should we commit suicide?" pool and the other toe was just like, "Yeah, hurry up already."

By the time I got back to school I was at rock bottom. I was back in my apartment with my four roommates, who were great, funny guys, but something was different. It didn't help that January in New Hampshire meant everything was cold, dark, and slushy. It's that time of year where the streets looked like a special truck followed behind the snow plow to spray mud all over them. The upbeat and charming visuals of the holidays were over, as was my outlook on life.

I caught myself staring at the wall for minutes at a time. Listening to somber music on my laptop. Saying 'maybe' to plans, then ultimately saying no by not leaving my room when it was time to go. My energy was not only down; so were my ambitions. The student film I was the producer on all year for my film production major, was done shooting and now in post-production. My duties had really quieted down. All I was required to do was show up to my normal classes and try not to freeze to death.

But a new task seemed to slowly manifest itself onto my to-do list: suicide.

I was so depressed that the 'S-word' started to creep into

my train of thought so organically and subtly you would think it was on Seal Team 6. I didn't dare mutter a word of these drastic and depressing thoughts to another human being. Especially not my family. Three sisters and one mother can be nurturing and fun and also a nightmare. I knew they'd get rightfully upset, then bombard me with helpful tips and positive thoughts causing me to run for cover and wish I had said nothing.

The day I started to brainstorm how I might kill myself is when my subconscious started to be concerned. I had decided that my family's house on Nantucket would be a good place to do it. It was perfectly remote and always had a special place in my heart. I didn't get into the details per se. I just had decided that I didn't like life anymore. Fortunately, while I was struggling to formulate a half-assed plan, a speed bump magically appeared.

I was on the phone with my eldest sister, Sami. She must've sensed my depression, my lethargic voice sounding lazier than ever. Or maybe it was just the lack of excitement going on in my life as a twenty-one-year-old who had no serious adult responsibilities and was surrounded by three thousand women. Whatever the reason, she said something that I annoyingly didn't see coming.

"You know we'd all be devastated if we lost you, right?," she said while we were on the phone. "We love you very much, and I don't know what I'd do if you were no longer around."

Woof.

It knocked the wind out of me. My ex, Sydney, had suggested therapy months ago. Sami's chat was the extra push I didn't want but needed. It was finally time I talked about feelings.

I found myself sitting on a Keene State College–issued loveseat that wouldn't win any awards for design but could have for comfort. I was so seriously worried about my mental health after continuing to stare at the wall and listen to Creed after I'd hopped off the phone with Sami that I had made an appointment through the behavioral health department on campus, which meant all sessions would be free. Outside the behavioral health building's window, snow flurries were falling, making the brown slush look quite picturesque. The kind woman seated across from me in her sofa chair and LL Bean sweater was not only my first therapist ever, but also the size of a chipmunk. There was an instant feeling of comfort, though, in that cozy den she had created in her office.

While my body was comfy, my emotions were not. Talking about feelings was like starting Level 1 Spanish. And this teacher wanted her only student to do the talking.

Sixty seconds of silence had easily passed. Maybe even seventy-five. Was I counting? Obviously yes. "What do we do now?" I muttered awkwardly. I felt stiff and tense.

The therapist smiled, yet no words came out of her baby-sized mouth.

"Okay, cool," I replied like a little ass.

"Say what's on your mind," she prompted me.

Oh, did she just speak? Thank god.

"Nothing's really on my mind," I said with an air of difficulty she was obviously experienced with. My therapist, bless her heart, was extremely patient. She had to be.

My family growing up was always very vocal. If someone hurt their back from moving a sofa or had an upset stomach from a plate of pad thai, you'd know about it. But expressing feelings didn't have the same TMI treatment, and growing up in the nineties, for men to have feelings was seen as lame. So for me at age twenty-one to finally be asked to talk about feelings was challenging. You can imagine how lucky my exes had been up until this point.

"I don't know how to do this," I admitted.

She gave another closed-mouth smile and stayed quiet.

"Do you wanna know why I'm here?" I asked.

She rested her head on her hand, which was her silent, patient way of saying, *no shit Sherlock, start talking*. I had to step up to the mic. There was no choice. I looked around the room again, feeling uncomfortable with the idea of making eye contact. My attention went to the snowfall outside. It was like watching a screensaver. I stopped thinking about what I should say and took my first step.

"My dad died a year ago. My ex and I broke up last fall. Life has been really dark lately. I've been really depressed, so people recommended I see a therapist, so here I am. It's my first time by the way."

The floodgate was now open.

She suddenly shifted and positioned herself so she had her legs crossed underneath her in the chair. She read the verbal cues as well as my body language: my mouth was moving and things were coming out. All of her years of experience had taught her one thing. I was ready to tango.

It took me a few sessions to open up. And more importantly to get used to the silence. Therapists are super awkward if you've never been to one. You'll soon learn their silence is crucial, but it goes against everything you're used to. Especially if you're like me and come from a chatty family.

That's the aspect I was appreciative of the most. For forty-five minutes once a week you have someone's undivided attention. No matter how empathetic a family member or friend can be, eventually they're gonna get tired of hearing about your troubles. Especially if the topic involves people they've never met.

I went to my first therapist once a week for the remainder of my senior year, which was about three months. It was monumental toward my recovery from depression. She got me to vent as well as notice why I did things the way I did them. Before therapy, I had had no clue that how my parents were raised had affected how they raised me. Basically if your grandfather sucks you're gonna pay for it in some form or another.

She also taught me to put ego aside and seek all forms of help, including antidepressants. I saw my doctor a week after she suggested this, when I was home for spring break.

I was still going to my pediatrician, so I was surrounded by small children playing with toys. The doctor was cool and I'm lazy when it comes to fixing boring details like going to a grownup doctor. Plus, it was nice to have blocks to play with while I waited to be seen.

"So, how can I help you today?" he asked with his usual, upbeat smile.

I was nervous to mention what I needed to mention. Basically I had a problem, and it was awkward for me to admit.

"I've been pretty depressed the past few months. I started seeing a therapist, and she mentioned that antidepressants can be helpful." Welp, guess it wasn't that hard. This was also the early 2000s where pharma ads had officially become approved, so every other commercial was for Prozac or Viagra. Doctors today might've treated me differently and not been so trigger-happy with the prescription pad.

My pediatrician clicked his prescription pen a few times. "Prozac is supposed to be pretty great. And it has minimal side effects," he enthusiastically stated.

"Wait, side effects?"

He smirked as he read the fear on my face. "It can suppress sex drive in men."

I wasn't having any sex, unless you counted my masturbation marathon over Christmas break. Women will say that doesn't count. Lonely men will disagree. "Will it make me less depressed?"

"Here's what antidepressants can be effective with." There was a dry erase board in the exam room, and he then drew a line on it going up and down in dramatic spikes. "This is how your mood can be now. When your day gets sad, your mood drops quite low. If something great happens, you might be *way* up here! Antidepressants can help even out those highs and lows." He then drew a line going across that was wavy but more or less calm.

I was sold. Before I knew it, I had a prescription in my hand for ten-milligram pills of Prozac. *EAT A DICK, TREVOR!*

I filled my prescription for happy pills, popped one down the old sad throat, and headed back to school already feeling better just knowing that stuff was coursing through my veins. Within two weeks, my mood had already drastically improved. I wasn't staring at blank walls anymore. A future without my father didn't seem great, but it seemed livable. Therapy was also becoming the comfort blanket I needed. It felt so good to bitch about how fucked over I felt that I had lost my dad so

120

young, and my therapist's overall warmth and positivity were contagious.

If winter was my cocoon of depression, spring was the beautiful emergence of the new me. I had my mojo back and was flirting with everything that walked. The Prozac boosted my confidence, and the women liked it. Ironically, though, the medicine that was driving my 'man whore' ways was also sabotaging it any time I got intimate with a woman.

"PLEASE JUST PUT MOM ON THE PHONE, SARAH!" I screamed into my Nokia flip phone. I had hooked up with a female friend the night before, and afterward it burned when I peed. Before you start judging like, *Gross, John has a dirty dick*, know that I wore a condom. I might be immature, but I'm not an idiot.

I called Pookie because, with her being a nurse, I thought she would know the next best course of action. I wasn't sure if she could have my doctor call in a prescription or if I was just supposed to go to the ER.

My bladder was getting full, and the idea of having a painful pee time again scared me into snapping again. "SARAH, HURRY THE FUCK UP!" I yelled. I was going to have to pee again, I just knew it, and Sarah's calmness was not only rare; it was also poorly timed.

"Geesh, calm down," Sarah snapped back. I was irate, which wasn't great, but she was not reading the room. My anxiety and stress were growing by the second. "What's the matter?" she then asked.

Sisters are great except when they're not. Like when they

feel the need to know everything going on because they're older and think they can solve any problem. "Sarah, for the love of god, please just get Mom before I scream!" That seemed to work because before I knew it Pookie was on the line.

"John, what the heck is the matter? Is everything okay?"

I was standing in the living room of my apartment. "This is really weird for me to say, but it burns when I pee."

"Oh, boy. From peeing? Or other stuff?," she shyly asked, more curious than concerned, I think.

"Other stuff," I said, embarrassed.

"Okay, just go to the ER. It could be a UTI. Hopefully it's not an STD."

"STD!" I screamed. "But I use protection!" *Now* I was pacing the room.

Pookie laughed.

"It's not funny!" I started to say, though I laughed too.

"Okay, sorry, sorry. Go to the ER. I'm sure it's just a UTI."

"Guys get UTIs?" I barked back into the receiver.

"Yes they can," said the ER doctor an hour later at the Keene Hospital. "Have you had any issues with urination lately?"

"Actually yes. I've been peeing a lot more this year than usual. Like two times before bed, which I never used to do. I'm on Prozac. Does that have anything to do with it? That's made my erections less erect, to be honest."

"It could be. Today we'll do the swab test to check to see if it's an STD, and then we'll send you home with some penicillin. You will then need to see a urologist to see if there is an issue with your urethra or bladder. I really think today it was a urinary tract infection, which now you know men can get too. Any questions?"

"Just one. Will the swab test hurt?" I asked.

"Yes," he said dryly.

I was confused how 'swabbing' something could hurt until I saw the weapon they employed for it. Now they can just test your pee for STDs, but in 2003 doctors, or at least the ones I was coming across, felt a long Q-tip inserted into a man's urethra was the best way to do the job. That's right. Q-tip right into the penis. I gripped the chair with both hands and literally hovered off of it an inch in response to the pain. The shock value was equally intense.

After I limped home, I put the new meds on my bureau and took a step back. My collection of prescription bottles all lined up across the top of my bureau was impressive at the time, yet alarming now, looking back in the present day.

Turns out it was a UTI after all. Go figure.

I've learned a lot from Trevor. Not just that men can get UTI's too—yay for equal rights—but more so I've learned how to deal with his froggy little ass when it resurfaces again. Which it does every year. Exercise, change of scenery, being social with friends and loved ones, and not beating myself up when something doesn't go as planned.

I think the biggest thing I've learned since that winter is that no matter how much an STD test hurts, it pales in comparison to the regret I'd feel if I had cut my life short, knowing what I've been able to experience over the past twenty years.

That's a level of pain that's immeasurable.

Although I'll never look at a Q-tip the same way ever again.

CHAPTER 11

LET'S GET WAY TOO PHYSICAL

I ARRIVED at the Cheshire Medical Center about five minutes late. Which was impressive for having funneled more than five beers the night before and going on less than five hours of sleep. Why I had agreed to an eight a.m. doctor's appointment is beyond me. And why I had never bothered to take the time to research what is involved in a prostate exam is also dumbfounding. In my defense, though, this was pre-Google. Plus my father never casually turned down music in his car and said, "Did I tell you about my prostate exam the other day? Man, they're a doozy! What happens is..." I was fifteen when he was first diagnosed. I didn't take cancer seriously. I had seen my mother go through it twice. No one dies in real life, I thought, just in movies. I also didn't think I'd be at risk for this type of cancer and need to be screened early on. So when my doctor from home insisted that I get the exam done and recommended a doctor I could see up at college, I didn't question it. I imagined it would just be like a physical. Just not *so* physical.

I was going in blind, and to make matters worse, I was extremely hungover.

I spotted a bathroom en route to the urology department and naturally ducked in quickly to relieve my bladder. Which was a rookie mistake for any doctor visit.

Again, I was twenty-two.

By the time I made it to the urology appointment, the woman at the front desk was already murdering me with her eyes. Her name tag read 'Sheila.'

"Hi, really sorry," was my opening line. "My name is John Col–"

She cut me off by slapping a urine sample cup on the counter. Sheila was *pissed*.

"We need a urine sample. You can use the bathrooms around the corner."

"Okay... I actually *just* went. Is that okay?"

She stared at me, expressionless.

I smiled nervously.

"Just try," she said with the least amount of effort possible. You would think she had climbed K2 the night before. Or had had the same night as me, where she partied like Def Leppard, then woke up so hungover that throwing up sounded like a vacation. Maybe she had family problems? We'll never know! Maybe she was just a nasty person!

"Okay, no problem," I replied to be polite and also because I was too scared to upset her.

I stood there, over the toilet, as not a drop of urine came out. I was in a single-stall bathroom, so privacy wasn't an issue. My recently drained bladder was. It wasn't like I had had chamomile tea the night before and was in bed lights out by nine. I had stage fright of the penis and the timing couldn't have been worse.

I shook a little to see if that would get anything going.

Nope, nada.

I exited the bathroom and found the nearest water fountain. I chugged as much as I could, then stood there. I thought the water would immediately rush to my downstairs area and tell my brain, "THIS MAN HAS TO PEE!"

I closed my eyes as if to make all my other senses sharper. *Talk to me, bladder. Daddy's listening.*

Radio silence. I looked toward the front desk. The warden looked up, and I immediately looked away, scared urine-less. I couldn't go back to her with an empty urine sample. She ran a tight ship. And fuck, was it really frustrating.

I chugged more from the water fountain. A nice gentleman walked by, and I rushed to chug more as if to say, "Fountain's taken!" He smiled and kept moving. He was so calm and happy. A pro. I bet he brought his own urine samples.

After three to four rounds of fountain chugging, my brain got the memo. It was pee time!

Moments later I approached the front desk, trying not to boast.

"Guess I really had to go," I jokingly said.

The warden didn't even flinch.

Can't blame her. I bet she hears that one all the time.

She sent me to the waiting room so I could read old issues of *People* and guess what was wrong with the other men's penises that were waiting with me.

. . .

Ten minutes later, as I sat in the examination room, my hangover decided to flare up again. It's like the bladder battle had completely distracted me from waves of nausea trying to make their way up my throat. I glanced at the sterile clock on the wall.

8:35 a.m.

I am technically a morning person. Though I hadn't had an eight a.m. class since freshman year, my usual alarm clock went off at that time during the week, and my usual sobriety level when it did was kosher. Today, though, I felt 'rode hard and put away wet' and was contemplating leaving the urology department altogether when the door creaked open and the silhouette of the doctor filled the frame.

"You must be John. I'm Dr. Askling," my urologist said as he closed the door and shook my hand. I was suddenly sitting on the edge of the examination table like a toddler waiting to get a Sour Apple Dum Dum. He shook my hand and proceeded to look at my file. No pleasantries. Or chit chat. This doctor was probably a blast at cocktail parties.

"Your father has prostate cancer?" he asked while putting on gloves.

"*Had* prostate cancer, actually. He passed away a year ago from it."

He stopped for a moment. "Sorry to hear that." Then he poured not just lubricant on his gloved right hand, but an *excessive* amount of lubricant. I was beginning to be alarmed. And for good reason.

"Okay, have you had a prostate exam before?" he asked. He

was assembling supplies when he did. Meanwhile, I was assembling all the triggers for future PTSD.

"I have not," I responded. An ounce of throw-up perked up in my stomach. Everyone but me was excited to see what was going to happen next.

"If it's alright with you, I'm going to perform a prostate exam. It's important to have this done maybe once a year. Usually not until you're forty, but it's good to do it now since there's a history of prostate cancer in your immediate family."

"Um, okay." It made sense, but the point of the gloves did not. Yet.

"Now please drop your trousers and underwear and bend over the table," he said way too casually.

Crap. That explained the gloves.

"Underwear too?" I asked, with a slight quiver in my voice. *God damn it, why hadn't I researched what this exam entailed?! It's not like when the appointment was made I had had a month to prepare!*

"Yes," he replied. "Underwear too."

That's when I glanced at his right hand. The fluorescent ceiling lights shimmered off the lube. *Did he put more on in the past minute?!* When I shifted my classes around so I had Fridays off, this was not what I'd envisioned I'd be doing with that spare time. Fridays in college were meant to be spent playing Nintendo 64 and eating cheesesteaks from the cafeteria. Not stripping down in front of a doctor who was armed with nothing but a lubed-up glove!

Navy Seals say the secret to overcoming stress, fear, and any other tough situation is to use the 'box-breathing' method.

You breathe in for four seconds, hold it for four, then exhale the same amount.

I prefer the 'rapid-joke' method, where I fire off dumb one-liners or useless comments as a defense mechanism in order to lighten the mood.

Dr. Askling stepped forward. "Okay, please place your hands on the table and spread your legs."

"You gonna buy me a drink first?" I joked.

He gave me the polite, no-teeth smile and stood there waiting for me to do as instructed.

I turned around and 'assumed the position,' but the dad jokes didn't stop. It was like a car crash in slow motion: slow enough that you felt like you could step in and stop it, but the reality was you not only couldn't but shouldn't. This was for my health. I think.

"You'd be really popular in some parts of Boston," I quipped.

He fully ignored that one. Meaning the jokes needed to end. But how?

Here's how.

He inserted his middle and index finger into my butt and proceeded to check to make sure my prostate wasn't enlarged. I was too uncomfortable to make even the smallest chirp of a bad joke. Having a doctor cup your balls while you turn and cough was amateur compared to this. This was Everest. Only there was nothing to celebrate.

Any time I complain about this procedure, the women in my life barely flinch.

"Welcome to my world, honey," they say. They are used to

a doctor putting his or her hand into their body. Sure, not the butt, and no, they don't enjoy it when it's done by their doctor, but my point is, something they are technically used to, a hand, is going into an orifice on their body they are used to, such as their vagina. Straight men? A hand in the butt is uncharted waters for most of us. (Not that there's anything wrong with it.)

If you ever feel like you have too much of a sense of humor and don't know how to shut it off, try having two cold, latex-glove-covered fingers go into your rear to turn you from Seinfeld to serious in .001 seconds flat.

He rooted around for what felt like twenty minutes. In reality it was about five seconds. He finished, threw away the glove, and handed me a box of tissues. I took them and paused for a moment. I then put my pants back on. I thought to myself, *What the heck are these for? To clean myself? I think only a shower will take care of that.* So then why the Kleenex box like I had just cried during a therapy sesh?

"They're in case you cum," Tim said matter-of-factly when I asked him later. Almost *too* matter-of-factly.

My jaw hit the floor. It was six months later, and I was living in LA. I had moved there months after graduation to put my film production degree to good use and 'make it big!' I met my friend Tim years prior when we worked at what has always been my favorite job: West Coast Video. We became friends instantly. He's smart, gay, and extremely funny. An incredible combo. He was casually making a Boboli pizza as I bugged him again in regards to his tissue explanation.

"WHAT DO YOU MEAN IN CASE I CAME?!" I yelled.

He burst out laughing.

"Well, c'mon, this is weird!" I prompted. "I need answers!"

"The doctor didn't explain that when the prostate is milked it can cause ejaculation?" Tim said as he put pre-sliced pepperoni on his pizza. Where others saw Boboli, Tim saw a masterpiece.

"Come to think of it, he didn't! He just said bend over and then that's when he put two middle-aged fingers up my asshole! Maybe next time he and I can have a cup of coffee first and really connect!"

Tim let out a big cackle and almost spilled the dumb jar of marinara sauce.

"What? Is that normal? Is that what happens with the gays?" I loved acting like Tim's sexual preference was like the Wild West or a foreign language that made no sense to me, and thus I mocked it often. He did the same to straight culture, so we were even.

He finally gave me his undivided attention. "If the prostate is milked, it can make a man orgasm. It can be done with fingers or even, say, a dildo."

My eyes went wide. I was quiet. Tim continued preparing his lunch but stopped after a minute and realized I had never replied.

"Wait, you didn't know that?"

Tim and I were both shocked for completely opposite reasons.

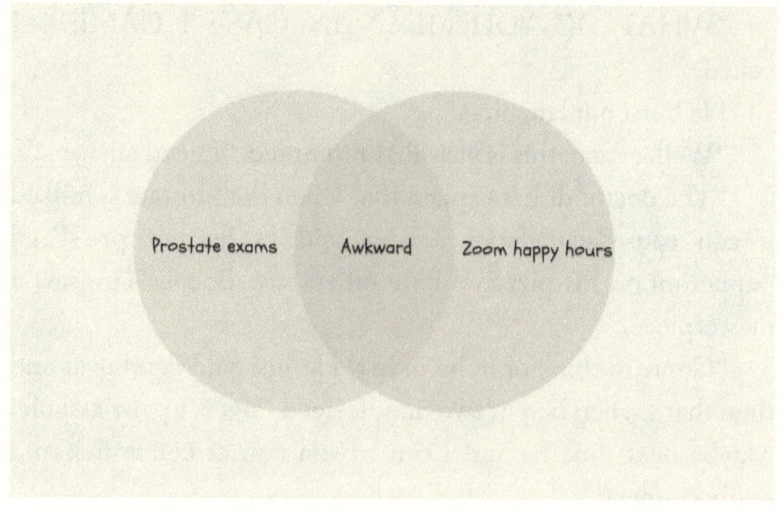

In the past twenty odd years I have had more than my fair share of prostate exams. Have I gotten good at them? Yes. Is it possible to get 'good' at doctor visits? Also yes. You are less nervous and know what to expect. Especially once you have more than five under your belt.

The irony of all these prostate exams is that this is not the only way to screen for prostate cancer. Men can also get a PSA test. According to the Movember organization: "If you have a family history or you're African American, do it at age forty-five. If you're fifty, do it now."

I saw a new doctor the other day and went over my family history. We naturally arrived at prostate cancer and how many exams I've had over the years.

"We have learned that we don't really need to do the rectal

exam annually. The PSA test, where we take blood to deter-
mine the measurement of prostate specific antigen (PSA)
concentration in the blood is good enough." Dr. Saleesi said.

Now they tell me.

STAGE 4: HERE THE FUCK WE GO

Put on your seatbelts. Time to introduce yourself as "The Trainwreck."

CHAPTER 12

THE STAND-IN

ONE UNEXPECTED PERK of losing a loved one that they don't tell you in the guidebooks is the free hand-me-downs. If you're a son and you lose a father, it's an all-around win because you've suddenly gained a whole new wardrobe. My father didn't technically hand me his old clothes. I just waltzed into his walk-in closet months after the funeral and raided the place.

The only problem was the age gap.

Suddenly I was back at college for spring semester, walking to class dressed like a middle-aged man. Brooks Brothers cashmere sweaters, khaki Dockers, even that goddamn Rainbow Fleet boat belt from Nantucket. Older women were beginning to notice me, and my friends were trying hard to do the opposite. I didn't care. My dad had great name brand stuff, and I was an unemployed student.

It freaked my sisters out.

"Is that Dad's merino wool long-sleeve polo?" Sarah asked

with a facial expression like she was watching someone put a cereal box away without closing it properly.

"Sure is!" I said proudly. We were at her baby shower. I needed something nice to wear, so boom, Dad's closet to the rescue.

"You wearing his stuff is creeping me out." She chuckled. We all did. But I could tell there was 80 percent truth to her joke.

Other friends came over wanting to get in on the fun.

Sami joined in.

"Dad's clothes again? John, don't you have any of your own?" Everyone chuckled.

I walked away, annoyed, and as I did, I passed by a mirror. Why did they have to give me such shit? If it was Mom who passed, they'd probably wear her stuff. I rotated to get a better view. This polo was really comfortable, let me tell you. Only problem was... yup...

I looked like I was taking my family to the country club for dinner because it was the end of the month and we had to 'make the minimum.' Not a great vibe.

Stepping into my dad's shoes didn't end at just the wardrobe. I had to fill in for him at my little sister's events as well. My father, bless his heart, was great at making my little sister, Natalie, be incredibly active despite having special needs and impaired vision in her left eye. But that got really annoying once he decided to die and I had to pick up the slack.

Take the Special Olympics swim meet Pookie made me attend with her. On a gray Sunday morning while I was home from college, Pookie, Natalie, and I trekked to what felt like North of the Wall, to a town in Massachusetts I had never heard of. It was also nine a.m., and at the age of twenty-one, anything before noon felt like a huge inconvenience.

I was of course wearing the yellow Tommy Hilfiger polo, but my outfit wasn't the focus of the day. The kids were. They had a swim team for every age group. It was impressive. It was also touching because most of the kids wouldn't have the social skills or confidence to compete on their public schools' swim teams, so it was nice that the Special Olympics had created a welcoming space for them.

Tired of the heartfelt talk? Me too. Want the reality of the situation? Here it goes.

This indoor pool complex had about four Olympic-size pools, so there was an insane echo of water splashing, parents trying to calmly yell, swimmers themselves making random noises, and just a radiant scent of urine throughout.

Curious about the noises? I was, too, until I met some of my sister's friends. They're like the X-Men. Everyone has a unique, special skill. With that skill might come a special tic or habit, but combined all the kids become a powerful unit.

Take Natalie, my sister. Sharp as a tack, with the memory of a Mensa member. The girl is like a Rolodex with phone numbers, appointments, and schedules. Forget a phone book. I got a Natalie.

Her friends bring other skills and unique traits to the table besides unconditional friendship. One girl jumps when she claps. Another screams instead of laughing. Chris's family has a beach house in Cape Cod. The skill sets and benefits of these kids varies greatly.

So when these kids swim, they aren't doing normal, boring

swimming like you're used to. These Olympics are special for a reason.

Suddenly there was a quacking sound from another pool. I thought someone had gotten hurt. Turns out a girl did really well in the freestyle race and the quacking was her way of expressing her happiness. Again, X-Men.

Not everything was announced via sound, though, that day. Some athletic accomplishments were silently achieved. I know this because moments after the duck girl quacked about her victory, I was staring off into the distance, daydreaming about god knows what when suddenly I realized the boy in my eyeline was ready to take home a prize I'm pretty sure they didn't have a category for.

Most Outstanding Boner.

It was like swimming was the last thing he came there to do that day. He just stood there in flip-flops, a Speedo, with a sundial in his pants. The balls on this kid—literally!

I nudged Pookie while trying not to laugh.

"Mom, look!"

She took one look over toward the young man, then turned back to me.

"Usually they all have 'em," she said matter-of-factly.

Not all the events where I had to stand in for Dad were as fun. Probably because some of them Pookie bailed on, so it was just me and Natalie, which was sadly our new normal.

It was June, just a few months after my dad had passed. Our town of Wellesley was having its First Day of Summer Concert kickoff party. My junior year of college had ended in

May, so I'd been home for almost a month and was set to leave for Nantucket in a few days to work for the summer. Basically my schedule was wide open. And I needed a break before watching *Happy Gilmore* for the sixteenth time.

"Natalie, talk to me about this concert. Is it gonna be lame?" I asked.

Natalie did her usual pitch to me where she is deep down very excited about something but tries to play it cool in front of me. "You know, I don't really know. But there will be fireworks, cake, and, you know, the Craigs might be going." Yup, Natalie was all jacked up.

"Mom, do you wanna go to the concert thingy?" I shouted upstairs. I believe my mom was on the phone with a good friend. The phone had always rung a lot because my mom is a social butterfly, but lately it had rung more than ever.

"I'M ALL SET, THANKS!" she yelled down like I was taking food orders. Not like I had yelled up, "Hey, can you come be a parent?"

I looked back at Natalie.

She was not going to break this cool-mode character bit she had going.

"You know, we could just stop by. If it's dumb we can leave. No big deal," she said.

I was amused but also annoyed. Thanks for dying, Dad! This kind of crap was his jam. He loved to take Natalie to events where he could talk shop with the other dads in the town, most of whom worked in Boston like himself. Some even worked at his law firm.

I let out a big sigh, then grabbed the keys to Pookie's 1998 salmon-colored Volvo station wagon, put on some cologne, and

Natalie and I headed to the dorky town concert. I, twenty-one and sluggish. She, eleven and blindly optimistic.

Ten minutes later we arrived. I turned off the ignition and spotted a mom already looking at us. She waved; I waved back. Then she half smiled like she was watching something sad take place.

"Natalie, who was that?"

"No idea," Natalie said.

This was already off to a good start.

We walked to the big baseball field where the event took place. Wellesley is an affluent town, so this wasn't like when the circus comes to town and the staff all look like they all share one toothbrush. This was much more pleasantly staffed.

Parents had volunteered to help, so there were MILFs manning the popcorn machines and DILFs selling raffle tickets, as happy families hunted for the best spots to plop down their blankets for when the fireworks went off.

Then there was us. It was like we had a scarlet letter on us, but instead of an 'A' for adultery, it was the letter 'E' for empathy. People would do drive-by's with little pats on the shoulders as they said, "Hey, so great to see you guys out!" Neither of us knew who they were. Natalie generally knows more people than I do in that town. She's heavily involved in our church, and she's amazing with stats and names, but this was even a bit much for her. She'd be trying to piece together a name, but then the next person was already on us with an empathetic look and sometimes even a hug.

The awkwardness grew as people would stop, say hello, and then ask where our mom was.

"On the phone, I think," I'd joke even though it was dead accurate.

We walked around the event, making sure to do a full lap. I bet my dad would've known a lot of people in the crowd, but it was also a younger parent vibe there, with most of them in their mid-thirties or forties. Everyone was like a full and happy family, and then there was Natalie and me, the odd couple. People didn't know what to make of us. Were we brother and sister? Father and daughter? Babysitter and client? Boyfriend and girlfriend? Who knows?!

A really nice older woman from our church came over. She said hello, that she hoped everyone was doing well. Then, like she had set a timer on her watch, after exactly sixty seconds, she was patting us on the shoulders and heading back toward her happy, grief-free family.

It was like, "There go the sad Colberts. Don't get too close—that shit is contagious!"

Right as a firework burst over our heads and everyone looked up in awe and excitement, Natalie and I looked around disappointed.

I nudged her arm. "This sucks. Do you want to leave?"

"Yeah. Mom should've come. She would've liked it." Natalie clearly was ready to stick it out longer. While I had fifty things to criticize, her only complaint was that Pookie wasn't with us. But I was twenty-one, selfish, and not emotionally mature enough to play Jack Colbert just yet—even if I was dressed for the part.

We slowly and calmly got up from our spot. We didn't even have a blanket. That's how unprepared we were. At least it made packing as easy as standing up, brushing grass off of our butts, swallowing our dignity, and heading for the parking lot without making eye contact.

I'll never forget how good it felt to open the car door and close it behind me and just live in the quiet cocoon of my mom's Volvo. A wave of relief washed over me.

"OH MY GOD THAT SUCKED!" I blurted out happily as I started the car.

Natalie, always my biggest fan, followed suit. "Yeah, did you see Mrs. Albany? She looked weird!"

"I have no idea who that is, but what I do know is that that was awkward."

I knew I could count on my little sister for unconditional support. She never judged my insecurities or dumb habits. Thank god too. I felt like the day couldn't get any worse. That's when I noticed her staring at me. She quickly looked forward as if she was guilty of something.

"What?" I asked.

"Nothing," Natalie said, playing it cool. "Just... is that Dad's shirt?"

CHAPTER 13
TAKE_IT_OR_LEAVEIT58

GRIEVING MAKES NO SENSE. You're tired all the time, yet you feel like you haven't done anything to justify it. When you run five miles or 'get swole' at the gym, you can hit a wall later in the day and it makes sense. *I need a coffee because I worked out earlier.* Or, *I've been in back-to-back meetings since eight a.m., and that's why I'm exhausted.* It all adds up.

Grieving is the opposite. You will have done nothing physical, yet you have the energy of an AARP member. Sadness is an invisible wonder. It washes over you like a slow wave that drains every ounce of energy out of you in the process. Wax on, wax off. Johnny sleepy now.

What's funny about the movies I saw during this stage was their level of quality. I was basically a slutty audience member. I would watch anything. I still do to a degree, but back then I had so much free time I could afford to not be picky. I just needed content.

I found myself watching bad movies with good people.

Like the time I rented *Unfaithful*, starring Diane Lane and

Richard Gere, for Pookie and me. It was the end of May in New England, humid as fuck, and I had nothing but time and she was in the same boat. My father had passed three months earlier, I had just finished my junior year at Keene State, and to escape life in general, my buddy and I were going to drive cross-country to intern in the entertainment industry in LA for the summer. We weren't leaving for another two weeks.

I always thought it was my dad who was the movie lover of that pair, but turns out the Pookster is a cinephile as well. When I told her that I had Diane Lane's new movie *Unfaithful*, she was psyched. *Under the Tuscan Sun* was her *Citizen Kane*.

"Ooh, baby, that works!" she chirped as she shuffled to the kitchen in fresh jammies to pour herself a glass of chardonnay and then plop some ice cubes into it. Always chardonnay, and always one cube shy of white sangria.

I turned over the VHS to read the synopsis on the back because truthfully I didn't know much more than that it was a drama/thriller and who was in it. Richard Gere was great in *Pretty Woman* and *The Day of the Jackal*, and Diane Lane was hot, so I was game.

I began to read the synopsis out loud as I pushed the tape into the VCR.

"A New York suburban couple's marriage goes dangerously awry when the wife indulges in an..." I paused for a moment, pretending I hadn't read the next two words. But I had and there was no going back. "....goes dangerously awry when the wife indulges in an *adulterous fling*."

Oh god what have I done?

Pookie didn't seem to give it a second thought as she curled up on one end of the leather sofa. She had wine and a movie.

She'd also gone through two rounds of breast cancer treatment and the death of her husband. Her present situation was heavenly by comparison.

We were thirty minutes into the movie when things got interesting. Richard Gere was seen less and less, and suddenly, after a sexy Italian artist helps Diane Lane hail a cab during a freak windy day in Manhattan, a week later she meets up with him for coffee to thank him. A cappuccino during the day. No harm in that, right?

WRONG.

This isn't a chance for Diane to take a break from being a busy mom to enjoy a mature conversation with another adult and a six-dollar cappuccino. This is a chance for Diane to do naughty things with a person who isn't her husband! *Under the Tuscan Sun 2: Momma Needs to Smash.* Unfortunately I was beginning to get that vibe because when Diane excuses herself to go to the bathroom, the sexy Italian follows her, and she doesn't stop him. Instead, she giggles. I didn't get up to leave the room like a sane person. I can explain.

Hollywood makes movies and shows to appeal to a broad audience. For the most part, leading men and women never get graphically killed or aroused. Last time I checked, no one is getting their back blown out on *Blue Bloods* on CBS.

So as Diane and the Italian started making out in the bathroom stall, and his hand went down her pants, I nearly spat out my beer. You can understand why. This was getting surprisingly graphic.

"Whoa, did that really just happen?" I asked, amused.

"Holy moly," Pookie chirped.

I was getting super uncomfortable seeing as my mother was

four feet away as Diane continued to get fingered on screen and I continued to watch. I couldn't look away! It was like a car crash except the cars were having sex! My defense mechanism of 'comment on the elephant in the room when feeling awkward' kicked in.

"What if someone needs that stall? Do they just wait until they're done?" I joked.

Pookie laughed, god bless her. She was focused on the scene, though, which was creepy in its own right.

Moments passed and we were back in the cafe as Diane, disheveled, having just had an orgasm at two o'clock on a Tuesday in a public restroom, takes her seat, tucks her shirt back in, and proceeds to sip her probably cold cappuccino. Like a cat who swallowed the canary, she can barely hold in her teenage giggles until the Italian comes back into the room and leans across the counter to flirtatiously get a napkin from the barista. Just before she hands him one, he does the grossest thing I've ever seen in a movie that wasn't a porn.

"He just smelled his fingers!" Pookie yelled out with a cackle.

I was speechless.

Diane was not. With a foam mustache on her pretty little upper lip, she suddenly let out a laugh, having witnessed this finger-smell as well and quickly looked around out of embarrassment.

Somehow no one in the café saw this.

WTF was this movie? But also how would it end? I refilled Pookie's wine, got myself another beer, and watched the rest of this steamy thriller while making random jokes during the sex scenes. The writing was legitimately good. You really felt for the characters. Diane Lane was cheating, but it was so enter-taining you didn't want her to do the right thing and end it. Richard Gere was a great husband, but he was basically just a quiet, boring guy in a cardigan in every scene, so it was like screw it, back to the naughty stuff.

As if the movie was listening to my brain, the 'lover' bent Diane Lane over in the hallway and just took her to the bone zone with no shame. It was hot. As in literally: Pookie and I were sweating like pigs thanks to my parents only installing A/C in the upstairs bedrooms. There I sat, stuck to the leather sofa from 90 percent New England humidity with my fifty-five-year-old widowed mother ten feet away from me, chugging icy chardonnay.

I was uncomfortable emotionally and physically. She was something else altogether.

She let out another cackle followed by a creepily quiet yet dramatic "oh my." It contained too much envy and not enough amusement. Why, oh why, didn't I rent *Minority Report* instead?

I want to tell you that now, at the midpoint of the film, fifty-five minutes in, I got off my ass and went to hang out with friends or read a book. Anything to improve my situation versus continuing to complain about it. I didn't. I remained stuck to the leather sofa thanks to the heat, but also because this widow porn was funny. Also, you have to understand, watching movies with Pookie is fun in general. Her brain reacts very quickly in real time to what's happening on screen and just blurts out noises and funny, short, made-up words to express her emotion, be it amusement, fright, shock, feeling charmed, or whatever.

Take, for instance, when Richard Gere asks Diana Lane where she was all day and she says, "Just out with a friend," and smirks.

Pookie let out an "Oh, that's rich!," then a "hmm."

This peanut gallery is entertaining. Sometimes she does it too often, but while Pookie and I sat there, both stuck to our ends of the leather couch on that balmy summer night in that great big house, we were bonding. The house was peaceful, and it was nice just hanging out with my mom. But there was a clear takeaway from the experience: my mother needed a man again.

And central air on the first floor.

After my father's passing Pookie suddenly found herself with weird new titles attached to her name like 'widow,' 'single,' and 'hoarder.' The last one was merely coined by us, her asshole kids, but that doesn't make it any less true.

After roughly three decades, Cheryl Colbert was back on the single train and ready to have fun again. For six years she helped take care of my dad while he fought cancer, with the last three months of his life being by far the hardest. They were happily married, and after doing all that she could for my dad, now that he was gone, it was time for her to focus on herself. She was ready to be adored again, and she deserved that. Especially if it included free dinners at Legal Seafoods.

That's when PJ came into her life. That's not his real name, but 'Post Jack' is a great, fake nickname that helps me avoid getting sued. I was a big fan of the guy. Sure, it was weird as hell seeing my mom hang out with a guy that didn't have double chins and didn't have my last name, but PJ was success-ful, charming, and took my mom to really, and I mean really, nice places.

When I say around the world, I mean it. Remember that cool plane that extremely successful business execs would take so they could fly to London *just* for a meeting and be back in time for dinner at Le Cirque? And that plane doesn't exist anymore because a few blew up? That's right. Pookie and PJ rode the goddamn Concorde. To Paris, no less! They drank pink champagne while Pookie literally chatted up the gorgeous, and apparently nice, Liv Tyler who was seated just behind them. She told Liv that her son was a filmmaker, so Liv gave her her autograph. (I still have it!) They flew to other places, too, but I can't remember them. Plus they can't possibly top 'Concorde to Paris.' But there were more first-class plane rides, four-star meals, and endless pampering for my mother. This was a fun time for Pookie, and while she didn't need my approval, she had it.

PJ seemed to have some 'complicated' stuff going on with his adult kids, the details of which I know nothing about. Truly, I didn't care. PJ wanted a fun copilot, and Pookie just wanted to run as far away as possible from grief and people feeling so sorry for her. It was love at first overpriced flight and I enjoyed it.

I'll be honest with myself. I was in new territory with my mother dating. She had been with my father for the past thirty-two years. My entire life. I had very mixed feelings about the whole thing. But PJ was a great transition boyfriend to get me used to this 'new normal.'

He bought my approval, not directly on purpose, but nonetheless, I was perfectly okay with that. He had similar traits to my father, which helped. He drove around in a nice, black Mercedes, he was a successful executive like my father, and he did nice things, like driving up with my mom to visit me at Keene State. He scored major points that day. He took us out to a very nice lunch, asked me a lot of questions in a way that indicated he wanted to know the answers, and laughed at all my jokes. Sounds like a simple formula, but it's rarer than you think. Am I a cheap date? Rhetorical questions are fun.

Like all good things, though, the PJ adventures eventually faded out. I think one of his kids was going through a tough time and my mom also started to need more. I think I was more bummed about the breakup than she was. It's like I had a bad gut feeling that Pookie had just peaked. Either because I had good instincts about dating as someone who up to this point had dated seriously about four women, or because the next guy said the full phrase 'Information technology' instead of just 'IT.'

Red flag #1.

"Match.com? No, thank you," Pookie politely yet negatively declined. We were all sitting around drinking coffee in our sweats one morning that following summer in Nantucket. The hangouts with PJ had officially ceased, and we all wanted Pookie to get back out there. She felt the opposite.

"Online dating is how women end up on the evening

news." She pursed her lips as secondhand tension rushed through her body.

We all laughed while also rolling our eyes.

I chimed in, slightly frustrated. "You won't get murdered. You can do research on every bachelor and only respond to the ones you like. Otherwise, how are you ever going to meet guys?" I said.

"I don't need to meet guys," Pookie whined back. "Besides, don't you need a screen name or something for those types of sites?"

"Ooh, this will be fun!" Sami shouted from the kitchen. Heaven forbid anyone in my family misses out on giving their opinion. Suddenly she was in the room.

"What do you put? Your first name?" Pookie asked.

"Yeah, but that's boring," I said. "Let's make it fun. Like Hoarder58."

Pookie glared at me.

"You like to dance. What about MomDancer58?" Sarah said.

"Stop putting my age in it!" Pookie blurted out.

"What's the place at the dump that you love where you can drop off old junk or pick up old crap? Like a NordicTrack or a crib?" I asked.

"Take it or leave it," Sarah said, amused.

"TakeItorLeaveit58! That's perfect," I said. I was trying not to laugh too hard at my own joke.

"Oh, stop," Pookie said.

Miraculously, a week later Pookie announced she got a match.

. . .

His name for this story is Gary. The name Pookie legit gave herself on Match was 58Dancer. The age made it in there, just none of the clever humor we had strongly suggested alongside it. Gary worked in 'Information Technology' as Pookie put it. Never IT. I suppose that was one way PJ had rubbed off on her. Gary would come over on Saturday mornings and surprise my mom and little sister with fresh pastries and other delectable, treats. Gary was very thoughtful, very kind...

...and the worst storyteller on the planet.

He was a slow talker. Not in the sense that his stories contained too many details. He put a half-second pause in between every few words. Sometimes between every word.

"...so your mother... was... on the dance... floor and she... turns to me... and says..." He paused while giggling and looking at Pookie.

Meanwhile I'm just like, "Get this story over with already."

My mother also has this bad habit with any boyfriend where she cues up stories that she's already heard, but her boyfriend hasn't, as if she's hosting a late night talk show.

"So, John, you and Charlotte went to New Orleans last week? How was it?" she'd ask in front of Gary after I literally told her all about it the day we got back.

On the flipside it was nice because it forced her to learn more about my life. Living in Manhattan at the time and me being a lame son and not calling her super often, she wasn't always up to date on my career, living situation, and so on.

Gary was no svelte athlete, but that bald-headed information-tion technologist could sure cut a rug. He and Pookie would go out dancing all the time. A lot of Irish bars in our area would have live music, and those two little idiots would tear 'em up.

For the brief two or three years that my mom belonged to the Sankaty Head Golf Club on Nantucket (after my father got in literally the day of his funeral), we all made sure to attend the Fourth of July party one summer. The dance floor eventually thinned out but my siblings and I sat tired in fold-up chairs as we watched Pookie and Gary stay on the dance floor like they drank the fountain of youth. While none of us thought Gary was 'the one,' we liked how he made our mom feel. And act.

For the previous ten years I had seen a pretty buttoned-up mother of four move about this world at 120 mph. We called her 'the Tornado' because she would fly through a room, with an arm full of soccer cleats, notepads, and the portable telephone. She'd ask a question, give a stern command, roll her eyes, and then spin out into another room. She didn't work a room; she mauled it.

Her youngest daughter was born with impaired vision, making her blind in one eye, and a nonverbal learning disability. Pookie also got breast cancer and survived it. Then her hubby got prostate cancer and didn't survive. She had gone through a lot. By the time she met Gary, this farm girl was ready to P-A-R-T-Y.

Like the night of Grandma Phyllis's funeral. While crabby on the surface, Phyllis meant well and could be a sweetheart. Plus, she wasn't like other grandmothers. She was a card shark, had a tiny butterfly tattoo above her breast, and drove a convertible. (Although quite anxiously as we recall when flurries were on the forecast). She was diagnosed with lung cancer in the balmy summer of 2010. The outcome wasn't looking good, and I got sad knowing that not only would my grandmother soon be deceased, but our Christmas traditions would be too.

The wake was down the street from The Vienna, a Victorian B&B whose owner my uncle Jay knew. Moments after the service ended, we found ourselves sitting on The Vienna's patio with candles burning and bottles of red wine flowing. Both my mom's brothers were there as well as their wives and children, including my cousin Danielle who is just a few years younger than me. Gary was there too. Pookie was giggly with him around and not mourning the death of her mother, which was nice. The woman has seen so much death that she's a pro at funerals. It's impressive and strange and a therapist's dream, but I'm not going to unpack that now.

After the mains had been cleared, and the illumination from numerous candles lit up our drunk smiles, I decided it was a good time to excuse myself to pee. I tend to hit the bathroom more often than a senior citizen; plus, I had about three bottles of Côtes du Rhone swishing around in my bladder. I braced myself and got up out of my iron patio chair and headed up the stone steps toward the inn, where the bathrooms were located.

I was drunk and content, weaving through the historical architecture of this fine establishment, following the hand gestures of a helpful passing waitress since clearly patrons are lost often, when something caught my attention out of the corner of my eye.

I darted my head dramatically to see it head on and get a better look, while my body continued forward. That's when my heart skipped a beat, and my shoulder nailed a doorframe.

"AW, FUCK!" I yelled out, then quickly looked around embarrassed. None of the diners in the surrounding rooms noticed nor did they give a shit. Thank god. I rubbed my shoulder and glanced back over.

My eyes weren't seeing things. The sight before me was in fact real. And why did it require an emergency double take and hitting pause on an overflowing bladder?

What I saw was Pookie and Gary up against the wall, passionately making out. It was like Gary had been overseas fighting in the war and hadn't seen "his girl" in two years. That's how passionate/gross it was. Like a pair of old, retired athletes getting back on the field for the first time in thirty years, they were sloppy, but you couldn't look away.

I hurled myself into the bathroom, and I peed as fast as I could. I might've sprayed all over the entire wall. I have no idea. I washed my hands in the old-timey Victorian sink and caught my reflection in the mirror. I looked like I had just seen a ghost. Or my mom French-kissing her 'lover.'

I had never seen her and my dad make out. Although I did hear them having sex once or twice over the years, which was gross, this was something else. It was obviously cringeworthy and hysterical, but as I stood there seeing double, it dawned on me that what I had just seen was in fact also… endearing? (That's right, John; you can say things are endearing sometimes. It's okay.)

But seriously. My entire life I'd seen my mother do many things. Cry in her hands when she thought I wasn't looking, scold me when I was being a 'nudnik,' stress over bills, but I hadn't truly seen her have fun in a very long time. This wasn't just fun; this was drunk, horny-teenagers-about-to-get-murdered-in-the-opening-scene-of-a-horror-movie fun. She was having a blast at her mom's funeral.

Talk about goals.

I exited the bathroom and let this heartfelt reflecting time wash over me until I heard a BANG from outside. JESUS, DID THEY TRANSITION TO THE PATIO?! It happened again, and this time rapid-fire. *Bang, bang, bang...* BOOM. I ran outside to the front porch of The Vienna, turned the corner, and looked down the flight of wooden outdoor stairs. Aunt Ellen was rubbing her knee in pain while my uncle Larry helped her hobble back to the table. Turns out she had fallen down about four to five stairs. Hence the four to five "bangs" I heard. The poor woman has had knee problems for years, and I imagine the ten bottles of French wine we drank didn't help. Guess everyone was going out with a bang that night, except for Grandma Phyllis.

The next morning Pookie and I both woke up, each in our own little twin bed in my grandmother's house, extremely sweaty and hungover. No A/C and tons of alcohol, what a delightful combo. We shared a room since Gary was at a hotel. We also shared a vintage fan that I had found in the closet. It was no match for New England humidity.

As Pookie ripped a fart followed by a "oh was that me?" I headed to the bathroom, super hungover while clearing my throat. Phyllis's bathroom just outside the primary was head-to-toe baby blue with shag carpet around the base of the toilet. There was a matching cover for the toilet lid. It was incredible.

I stood over the toilet and cleared my throat again this time, louder and grosser. I thought I was alone.

I was wrong.

"Jesus, are you done?!" Sami yelled. In a daze I turned and looked out the bathroom window. There was a tent in the back-yard, which Sami's family had slept in because her boys thought it would be fun. I guess sleeping ten feet from the only bathroom wasn't.

Neither was Pookie's courtship with Gary. They broke up months later from no ill will just each had different needs at their respective grief journeys of their late partners. She found a new man a year or so later, and they've been together ever since.

I think he finds us all insane, but at least he can tell a story in under four hours.

CHAPTER 14
DATING WITH A DEAD DAD

THE GIRLFRIENDS I had along my grieving journey, from my father's diagnosis onward, had to put up with a lot with me. Especially once my dad's cancer got worse.

Sydney was sitting by my side at the rehab facility where my dad was trying his hardest to walk again after surgeons operated on the tumors on his spine. We were in his room all sitting around for a Sunday visit when Pookie started to move to the beat.

"Oh, I love this song," Pookie said.

"I Hope You Dance" by Lee Ann Womack was playing on the boombox my mom had brought in from home. She turned it up. We were laughing at her dorky dance moves when Sarah alerted us.

"Mom," Sarah said.

We looked over and saw that Dad was crying. I mean, could you blame him with *those* lyrics?

Pookie tried to keep dancing to cheer him up. It didn't work.

Sydney stuck around after that fun-filled day, but she was also there the day six months later, long after his funeral, that I discovered the angry stage of grief. We were living together our senior year of college. It would be months before I'd take her advice and actually see a therapist. Instead I'd tell her I was fine and didn't need to talk to someone about my anger.

"WHERE THE FUCK IS THE SCREWDRIVER?!" I'd scream.

"John, it's okay, calm down," she'd say. "Is it in the drawer in the kitchen?

"THAT'S A GODDAMN PHILLIPS-HEAD!"

I was single a month later.

Some people can be so sensitive.

Charlotte and I met when I was new to New York City at the ripe age of twenty-five. We worked at the same advertising agency and flirted at work happy hours and parties. Charlotte got the worst of my grieving adulthood. As the years rolled on I was becoming more in touch with my feelings and unpacking the trauma from my dad's death while also slowly developing a new sense of anxiety as I realized I wasn't getting any younger and my dad's age at his passing (fifty-six) was getting closer and closer with each birthday.

This made me indecisive and doubtful. I was comfortable with Charlotte day to day, but I wasn't sure about getting married to her or if I even wanted to get married in general. I didn't want to make the wrong choice when life felt so short. I didn't want to waste a minute of it. She brought up marriage often. Who could blame her? She wanted kids. And to know if we had a future.

I just wanted the F train to not get delayed.

There was a moment in our first year into dating when I sensed a red flag. A small signal that this was perhaps not a fluid match. But I was twenty-six, lived in a shithole apartment in the East Village, and felt like I was lucky to be dating anyone at all, let alone Charlotte.

We were in Mexico at an all-inclusive resort. We were sitting across from the Concierge at the hotel trying to pick out of a brochure, an excursion to do the next day. Colberts are annoying. We want to vacation but we can't just sit around all day or we get stir crazy. We need to be active one half of the day, then lazy the other. The problem was Charlotte and I couldn't agree on an activity.

"Ooh let's do the nature walk." she said.

"What about the ATV riding!" I'd blurt out.

"Are there snakes? Along the route?" She asked the Concierge.

He nodded, almost ashamed as if he already knew from that single question that that activity was dead on arrival. (Charlotte had an insane fear of snakes).

We kept flipping through the catalog of choices. Tired from our flight we decided to revisit this the next day. We had plenty of time although we never booked an excursion and I found myself getting bored with laying on the beach for five days straight. While it sounds like a ridiculous test to measure a life partner, I was disappointed in how that turned out. She was holding me back from adventure. We were in a beautiful place yet I left that trip feeling like we didn't take full advantage of it.

All my photos were of us drinking on the beach, or drinking at dinner.

While compatible, we also were on different pages. I loved Brooklyn but wanted to constantly get away on weekends, or eventually leave New York altogether. She was very content with exploring the neighborhood every weekend. And possibly for the next twenty years. But complacency does things to you. As does low self-esteem. You begin to think you can't do better, or better doesn't exist. So I stayed with her out of comfort. Minus the uncomfortable convos about marriage, our setup was quite posh. We would go out to dinner, bitch about advertising, and then enjoy puttering around shops on the weekends after brunch and in between hours of talking shit about the people on *House Hunters*. In our sixth year of dating, with the marriage topic inserting itself almost weekly, I had no choice but to finally start to see a therapist again. Figure out what "my problem" was.

I asked if she would see a therapist too.

"What for?" she asked.

"Because maybe it would be helpful for you as well?"

She smirked.

Months later after weekly therapy, and friends telling me Charlotte was awesome, I did the unthinkable.

I bought an engagement ring and asked her to marry me. She said yes.

Everyone in my life was happy for us. I felt relieved. I was done contemplating. I made my decision. But when women gushed over Charlotte and asked "Are you so happy?!" she replied as if she took a new job solely for the salary. Truthfully I think she was nervous that my heart wasn't in it. Charlotte was right. This was the obvious next step; this was what she wanted. Notice the absence of love there? We had become amazing roommates, compatible in so many ways, but something ultimately was holding me back.

I wasn't ready for kids. At least not just yet. I still wanted to give LA a go for career goals of writing and directing films, and I knew how demanding a career that can be. Especially on families. Also, was this person "the one?" What has the dating scene been like since I left it eight years ago? This all-you-can-eat-buffet of feelings and ambition translated to one thing: subconsciously I wasn't ready to settle down and was ignoring that fact. Comfort and fear were keeping me locked into a sure thing, but one day in therapy I just snapped. My therapist was chattier than usual, asking me completely normal wedding questions but in rapid fire:

"Will you write your own vows?"

"Who will your groomsmen be?"

"Will it be in Boston or New Orleans?"

But I felt overwhelmed and emotionally backed into a corner. So I snapped.

"I don't want to marry my girlfriend!" I blurted out.

We both sat there, stunned.

The next day I called the whole thing off. Very good friends thought I was making a mistake. I was scared of the future, but when you come to the decision to end things, you know that feeling is never going away. I had to do all the awkward, uncomfortable things if I didn't want to live with it hanging over my head. Including cancel the wedding venue and help Charlotte find a nice female roommate to replace me.

I felt like a piece of shit, but I knew in the long run we'd both be better off. I had flipped my fear so that instead of being scared that I could only do worse, I was now excited that the best was yet to come. I was ready to carpe the fuck out of the diem. I hadn't been single in almost a decade. With a 325-square-foot bachelor pad and a sick pair of custom orthotics, I was ready to hit the town. After all, I was in a city with 8 million people, at least half of whom identified as female.

I was ready to slay.

Correction: I was ready to sob. Three weeks into my bachelor days and I found myself bawling my eyes out when one of the old guys peacefully died sitting on a chair in *The Best Exotic Marigold Hotel*. It was two p.m. on a Saturday, and I was thirty-two. Yikes. Had my ambitions backfired? I took charge of my life and suddenly found myself crying uncontrollably to an old person rom-com. The fridge was stocked with Bud Light Lime, the dresser was stocked with every condom brand imaginable, yet here I was single, sad, and not loving every minute of it. I had to get my mojo back. I also had to find out when *The Best Exotic Marigold 2* came out.

"Jameson?" a cute girl asked. I had met her seconds ago when we were both standing at the bar, trying to get the bartender's attention.

"Like on the rocks?" I asked.

She laughed, thinking I was kidding. I was not. I had just gotten out of a serious relationship, where my ex and I routinely went antiquing on the weekends. If we ever did a shot, it was a shot of Robitussin because we were sick. I had done my best to get out of the apartment and away from sad old people movies, but I was thirty-two going on sixty-two in that bar. Everyone had so much energy! Didn't anybody around here work? I was like the old guy in *The Shawshank Redemption* who gets out of prison and is shocked to see gas-powered cars. I had some catching up to do.

I clinked my shot of whiskey with the coed and tipped it into my mouth, pretending to be comfortable. My chest felt warm. I suddenly felt like a frat boy again. And weirdly, alive. I was so busy being on this high that I didn't notice the girl was already gone and the bartender was waiting for me to sign the eighteen-dollar check.

I started to get phone numbers as I got better at doing shots and better at staying awake past ten p.m. The problem was the flirty girl I got the number from was not the same girl it felt like I'd text a week later to hang out. One night when one actually texted me back, even though it was late, I flew out of bed to respond.

Hey, it's Jess. You up?

AM I?!

You know it, I responded.

This is weird but can I use your bathroom? I'm at a bar nearby.

I nearly dropped the phone trying to respond as fast as possible. We were going to have sex that night. I could feel it.

. . .

I felt something else an hour later–the plunger starting to give me a blister as I worked to unclog the toilet. When Jess arrived, she had a burrito the size of a cat from a nearby bodega. She ate it while we chatted, then excused herself to use the bathroom. Ten minutes later she peeked her head out, embarrassed.

"Um, I think I screwed up your toilet."

Well, maybe you shouldn't have had a five-pound chicken, beans, and cheese burrito at eleven p.m.! I thought, though I kept that to myself. I helped her get a cab, then walked back inside, closed the door, and made a pact with my poor toilet: The next girl to come over needs to be one that I'm dating.

The dating apps were like the Island of Misfit Toys. Everyone I could land a date with was someone I immediately didn't want to be on a second date with. For eight months I put myself through the gauntlet of dates hoping to find someone great. Instead I found...

...out what it's like to get stood up. I did have two of the best old fashioneds of my life while sitting there in sadness.

...what it's like when a girl is easily six years older than her pics. A lot of wear and tear can happen in six years. I should know. My beard is lush and brown in old pics.

...that just because their profile is written in perfect English doesn't mean they'll be able to speak it. She was beautiful and could literally talk Thai, but she couldn't speak "witty banter" so it was a hard pass.

Every date felt like a formal job interview too, or else like a game of tennis where if you answer wrong, you lose. A question I'd hear on every single date was "Any fun trips planned this year?" Like, was Bumble giving girls emails laying out tips and tricks for their dates? And was that question at the top? I heard it every time! It was like a lead-in to see what we had in common: Have we both traveled to cool places? Am I wealthy enough to go to nice places that I can then take them to as well? What are my views on marriage? Politics? Bravo TV?

All of those were fine, though. It was a low-key one that always seemed to ruin the vibe.

So, what do your parents do?

Year one I'd make it easy. "They're retired in Massachusetts."

But by year two in the dating game I didn't have the energy to filter anymore. Nor the desire.

"My mom is retired and my dad is dead," I'd say in response, amused. I mean, how else do you say that to a complete stranger at a dive bar where just ten feet away someone is trying to not throw up the cheap tequila shot they just took?

"Oh," one girl said, then awkwardly picked up her phone to read a text.

Ouch.

That was it, the date was officially over. Opening up like that and having it be an epic fail stung a bit if I'm being truthful. The more I responded with the truth either in a sincere way or an honest way the easier it got though over time. It turned out to be a great litmus test.

If the girl was sympathetic it was a good sign. "Oh my god, I'm so sorry for your loss."

Too sympathetic could be annoying long term. "Oooooh nooo. I'm sooo sorry" one girl said as she kind of made a scene and wouldn't let us talk about anything else. Dare I say she cared too much?

I grew numb to how great, grand, or gross the responses became. I was comfortable with my grief. If others weren't, they could fuck off.

My search filters were growing increasingly specific as I dated my way from Manhattan to Brooklyn. Now in my thirties I was too tuned in to my feelings, to what I wanted out of a partner, and from all that I had experienced with two parents having cancer and one dying from it, I had a low tolerance for people that were unappreciative or worse–spoiled.

Hey, we all complain about mundane shit. It was when it was related to their two living parents that I couldn't really tolerate it. Or worse, they didn't want to hang out with them.

"When was the last time you were home?" I'd ask.

"I can't remember," one woman said. I wanted to dive into that more.

"Is it a sensitive topic? Did something happen?"

"Not really" she said so matter of factly. Then her ears perked up. "Hey they have Skee-Ball!"

For the record, I was not making this topic out to be a deal breaker. I was much more open-minded than that. You have to be when you're dating as an adult. But sadly, and yes, I say sadly, it felt like I needed more than just looks.

Getting old sucks.

Having had this realization about what I needed in a partner, I said fuck it to the dating apps and joined an intramural soccer team instead via Zogsports. I didn't do it intentionally to meet a mate. It was more to push myself to possibly make new friends and get back into a sport I had loved my entire childhood. But wouldn't ya know, a year in, a brunette with bangs who had played D1 for Syracuse showed up for one of our games on Roosevelt Island. To say Jill was really good on the field was an understatement. To say I was really awful was not. But after our first game together we naturally chatted it up; she was working at Crate & Barrel as a merchandising manager (training for what eventually would be her booming career in interior design), and I had just purchased one of their loveseats. You can analyze compatibility all you want, but sometimes all you need is a stupid couch to get the convo rolling. Jill made it easy. She actually texted me and responded if I ever texted her. Novel concept, right?

We slowly took our conversations from text to in person and found them veering towards the clichéd dating questions, which was something we both wanted to avoid at all costs. So with the safety off, I pulled the trigger and playfully revealed info. I went with my gut which told me she'd see the humor in it all. Casually hanging out or not, why waste my time with this seemingly great girl if she was going to respond poorly the way other dates had. I was 15+ years into grieving and no longer insecure about the whole thing.

Plus I was hammered.

We were holding hands, walking down Avenue A at one a.m., after dancing with friends at Beauty Bar. This is usually the part of the evening where I might have one last drink or go for a dollar slice before heading home, but this time, I tipsily shot my shot.

"My mom is retired and my dad is dead," I said. It was the

first time we started to hang out outside of soccer. I wasn't trying to sabotage things, I just had a good gut feeling about this girl.

"Oh man" she said.

I take that back. My gut sucks. Will she reach for her phone? Say she has to get up early tomorrow and ask for the check? *It was fun while it lasted,* I said in my head.

She kept her brisk walking pace and after a beat blurted out "Well my brother is a former drug addict!"

We both burst into laughter and continued whatever this version of speed dating was as we held hands like two little kids. Jackpot, baby.

My dad would've loved her, that's for damn sure. "She's athletic, she's funny, and she won't slow you down," he most likely would've said.

Jill was not only close with her family and parents, but she also didn't clam up when my dead dad came up. In fact she would purposefully ask questions about him to see if I'd cry.

Would your dad be proud of you?

What would your dad think about this restaurant?

I wonder what your life would be like if your dad was still alive.

I'd start to cry while answering these gems at dinners out. God bless the darkly lit restaurants of the East Village, which prevented other tables from seeing it all go down. We'd then laugh. Jill's parents both had had cancer and survived; plus, her brother had almost died as a kid, then was in and out of rehab for years because of it. She had experienced heavy stuff, and that was a nice bond between us.

Plus, she never clogged my toilet.

CHAPTER 15
A MEMORIAL GOLF TOURNEY THAT WAS DEFINITELY MEMORABLE

AFTER MY FATHER DIED, my sisters came up with the thoughtful idea of holding a golf tournament in his honor.

This would have been a great idea to honor someone who maybe played golf five to six times a year and mostly just for 'funsies,' but for Jack Colbert, it felt as if it was the *only* way we could honor his legacy. The man was obsessed with golf. So much so that when I turned eleven he had me start caddying at our country club; that way, he had another reason to drive there every Saturday morning. Plus, he was a caddy as a kid, so he just wanted me to follow in his footsteps. The problem was, I just wanted to nap. Hence our fifteen-year rivalry. Regardless, he adored the game of golf. It made him happy, it let him be social, and he took great joy in teaching others how to play it.

He was often ecstatic on the golf course. You'd be walking, carrying your bag, or pulling it on some old man cart, annoyed that you just lost your fourth ball on the second hole. But Jack Colbert would be happy to have the company while playing the sport he loved. He'd turn to you and go, "Does it get any better than this?" And you'd chuckle and say, "No, Dad, it doesn't." Or if you were me and fifteen you'd respond like a little shit with a line like, "Yes, it does get better than this! It's called lying in a pool!" He'd then try to playfully hit me or just roll his eyes.

Does it get any better than this? is a phrase my entire family has never forgotten. It helps you realize that something is better when you look back on it, so you might as well praise it when you're in the moment.

The first year of the Jack Colbert Memorial Golf Tournament was as premium as it gets. It was held at a prestigious private club in a wealthy suburb outside Boston. It was such a hit that they made it an annual event. While they have all been great, it's the fourth annual that is when things got *real* memorable.

Meet the Wayland Country Club. Don't let the name fool you. It's open to the public and open-minded when it comes to the stuffiness of golf. Primarily because at Wayland they have the one thing that many private clubs would never dare feature.

A beer cart.

They're also a great establishment because they agreed to let my family host the second, third and fourth annual Jack Colbert Memorial Golf Tournament there.

In 2015, Jill and I were in our first year of dating, so life was simpler, everything felt newer, and we were enjoying experiencing new places and things together. My advertising career in NYC was thriving, my father's death was more than ten years behind me, and for once the women in my family welcomed the person I was dating with open arms.

Sami had the hospitable idea to have Jill play in the tournament.

"She can play in one of the girl foursomes I'm putting together. Leah, Sue, and other people you've met. It'll be fun," Sami said.

"I don't think she's ever played golf before," I explained.

"Remember when we rented stand up-paddle boards in Florida?"

"Yeah."

"Remember how Jill was practically bored maneuvering the board while I was so shaky I almost crashed into a dock? She'll be fine," Sami said.

"Point taken."

I knew Jill could handle her own, athletically. What I was more anxious about was how she'd fare against my extended family, tone-wise. She grew up in a big family. But the wildest they get at functions is they throw bread. Whereas we throw sex jokes. Plus we had 'the cousins.' Composed of three women, all in their forties and daughters to my uncle Fred and aunt Judi, Chris, Nikki, and Stephanie are the most down-to-earth people on this planet and also the most unfiltered people on the planet.

When an outsider comes in, they can be very hands-on. Literally.

At that first annual golf tournament, it was my brother-in-law Jonathan that was the new kid on the block. When Sarah approached and happily said to the group, "Everyone, this is my boyfriend, Jonathan," and Aunt Judy said, "It is so nice to finally meet you," Stephanie flashed her beautiful, Julia Roberts–like, big smile and said, "Sarah asked me to not do anything embarrassing." As everyone laughed, she clenched both of Jonathan's nipples with her thumbs and index fingers and proceeded to twist back and forth, clockwise and counter-clockwise. It was her fingers versus his innocent nips, with nothing but a thin layer of golf polo between them. She took those nips for a test drive.

Sarah was mortified that she had just become immediately single. They hadn't been dating that long, and she was still in that 'I can't fuck this up' stage. But it all worked out. Jonathan loved it and now they're married with two beautiful kids, and his nips eventually healed.

Now three tournaments later, my date was the new kid.

Guard your nips Jill.

Cut to me now at the Fourth Annual tournament with a girl that I really liked and vivid memories of how much fun dating in New York City can be. Fortunately as we pulled into the Wayland Country Club it was Friday and a beautiful seventy-five degrees out. The sun was shining, and as I turned into the parking lot, a good friend of one of my sisters, was sitting on his car bumper, lacing up his golf shoes with the biggest smile on his face. I put my window down, which might've been a mistake.

"Johnny C., you little slut!" he yelled. An old guy walked by and gave us, one by one, a look. I laughed and so did Jill. We were off to the races.

"Uncle Fred!" I yelled. Standing with his back to the small bar in the clubhouse, which would have been at home back in 1985, was my dad's 'Irish twin,' Fred Colbert, born ten months before my dad. Uncle Fred is like Santa Claus. He's big, he's jolly, and he oozes unconditional love. He's like a heated blanket that never turns off. Plus, when he laughs, his shoulders go up and down like a cartoon character.

"John, good to see ya," he said as he gave me a big hug.

"Uncle Fred, this is Jill," I said while stepping aside to introduce him to my girlfriend.

"Jill, so nice to meet you. Would you like a Cape Codder?"

Yes, it was only eleven a.m., but hey, how often do you get to play golf in honor of your deceased brother? Plus, Fred was perfectly positioned at the clubhouse bar, and the bartender, who looked like she was an extra in *The Departed, was* losing her patience.

Jill laughed while looking nervously to me, then to Fred, then back to me.

"It's vodka and cranberry juice. You'll like it," I said, slightly nervous.

Like a shy field mouse Jill gave a quiet 'thank you,' then sipped one out of a plastic, fog-colored cup. I got myself a Corona, and the three of us toasted with our drinks. We were off to the races, but apparently we had catching up to do. Suddenly we heard a loud, shrieking cackle of laughter from one of the tables across the way.

Kathy McGraw Bentley, a good friend of the family, was doing Fireball shots with a table full of complete strangers. I don't even know if they were there for our tournament. They might have just been raging alcoholics that occasionally played golf. Kathy is a gem and apparently at this moment was no longer sober. This wasn't *going to* be a shitshow. It already was.

An hour later everyone that was playing golf was gathered around, ready to be assigned golf carts. I knew 70 percent of the guest list, so I was having a blast. There were friends of the family, actual family, even friends of my sisters I'd gotten to know over the years every time I came home for an event. During my euphoric state of "Yay, I know everyone" I had forgotten that Jill practically knew no one.

I suddenly found myself frantically running around looking for her, like a mom at a mall who thinks her child has been kidnapped.

"JILL?! Jill!" I called. "Has anyone seen the cute brunette I came here with named Jill?!"

Mere moments away from having a stroke, I noticed her chatting it up with some of the women from her foursome. Her straw was hitting nothing but ice at the bottom of her empty Cape Codder.

"Having a good time?" I smiled as I came up next to her.

"Sure am!" Jill exclaimed. Just then my Uncle Fred came over.

"Jill, would you like another?" he asked.

Before I could even laugh at the fact that Fred was handing out Cape Codders like Tic Tacs, Jill flashed him some finger guns and said, "You know it, Freddy."

Uncle Fred didn't expect it, but his shoulders started shaking and he was loving it. He chuckled and handed Jill a fresh refill.

My watch read twelve p.m.

Welcome to the Jack Colbert Memorial Golf Tournament.

With every golfer primed thanks to alcohol, the tournament kicked off with foursomes loading up onto carts and heading to their assigned holes. My foursome was just a threesome, but it was a well-curated threesome at that. I had 'Scotty Too Hottie,' a fraternity brother from college who, like Sami's friend Rob

Rose, was unfiltered but full of kindness. Then in our second cart was my bestie, Greggy. We grew up on the same street, and while our friendship didn't really take off until middle school, he would go on to be the best man at my wedding. We're the sort of friends where we cannot see each other for literally years but pick up where we left off in an instant. This is largely thanks to our shared sense of amazingly dark, self-deprecating humor.

I helped Greg put his bag on his cart, then threw myself out of the way as two carts flew by with drunk, laughing house-wives on it. There had to have been five women on one cart. It looked like Noah's Ark, where every pair of animals was squeezed together on the top deck. This was Jill's group—not a foursome as is standard. No, this was seven, forty-year-old moms who were far from their parental duties and extremely close to unlimited alcohol.

"I hope they don't die," I said to Greg as he began to fill out our scorecard.

He seemed to be concerned about matters closer to home.

"I hope I don't shit my pants," he muttered. He looked like his stomach wasn't reacting well to the charred burger he had eaten way too quickly at the clubhouse.

Suddenly the eighty-five-year-old golf course ranger screeched to a quick stop right beside my cart. I nearly had a heart attack.

"You guys need to get to hole eight, now," he barked, then zipped away to go yell at someone else.

I was about to be stressed until a Corona clinked my beer.

"Cheers, bitch," Scotty said.

I clinked back, and we both took swigs. The tourney had officially begun! I floored the gas with my 1995 Footjoys.

Away we went at a top speed of 20 mph.

Eventually Jill hopped into our group. We had the room, and we knew it would be fun.

"How was the girl gang?" I asked her as I drove us to the green. Greg, being the gentleman that he is, had Scotty join him in his cart so Jill and I could ride together.

"Comical," Jill replied. "I was cracking up."

"Watch this," I said. By the way, anytime someone says, "Watch this," they are about to do something stupid.

I hit the brake and slid a bit on a wet patch of fairway. I chuckled. The five Bud Lights clicking around in our cooler were taking effect, and I was in a happy, reckless mode.

"Dumb," Jill said with a slight smile and a shake of her head.

It was nice having Jill in our group. Seeing as she was an extreme beginner to the game of golf, we were all able to give her tips, and without a care in the world, we were able to be patient with her as well. It was eighty degrees out on a Friday, so what else did we have to do? Plus Jill was a college athlete. She can pick up a hockey stick at the wrong end and say, "This is hockey?," then slap the puck 900 mph towards the goal. I liked having her by my side.

That is, until my second "Watch this."

There's a cart path at Wayland Country Club that takes a hairpin turn toward the tee box after you finish the previous hole. It winds around a nice little pond that is stocked with a crane and some dumb frogs. It's quite lovely, actually. The only thing that could ruin it, is if someone should press their foot heavier on the pedal because they've been drinking and their judgment and ego has been effected. If you do this, you might find yourself approaching the sharp turn about 15 mph faster than the ranger would strongly advise.

If you're like me, or anyone else who loves alcohol, your judgment changes and your ego soars when you're on the stuff. That sounded like a huge red flag, but don't worry, my drinking is nothing to worry about. My golf cart driving skills, now that's a different story. Combine my love of booze with driving golf carts, then subtract the skill I have divided by me being happy with a pretty girlfriend by my side and suddenly this happens.

I gripped the wheel with a sly grin, turned to Jill, and said: "Watch this."

To which she replied: "Oh god."

Before she could even grip the cart's side handle, I threw all my strength into my forearms and turned the wheel to the left so hard and fast that the whole cart turned before our bodies did. Jill, being on the side of the cart, taking the longer distance on the turn, quickly found her buttocks lifting out of the seat against her will.

In a slow-motion sequence Jill flew out of our golf cart, still upright, and because she is an athletic freak of nature she twirled in the air. I kid you not. TWIRLED. Like Tonya Harding doing a triple axel. I noticed out of the corner of my eye and looked over and just said in super-slow gibberish: "OHHHH NOOOOOO."

As the cart turned, I couldn't take my eyes off Jill. Her coordination was uncanny. What she did was so breathtaking I slammed on the brakes so it could have my full attention. In doing so my gut hit the steering wheel, causing me to come very close to throwing up a hot dog and what felt like a thirty rack of Bud Light. Now a normal person would've landed on their ass, or worse, their head. They would've screamed, then bled, then decided at that moment they'd very much like to be single again.

Praise the lord that Jill wasn't born normal. Or a mortal.

She didn't fall.

She literally did a 420-degree turn in the air, then gracefully pirouetted upon landing to absorb the shock. She looked at me in complete bafflement. Maybe because I had just thrown her out of a golf cart or maybe because she had landed the jump so perfectly. Probably more the former than the latter.

One thing was definite. I felt awful.

But in case I didn't, my family was nearby to help convince me.

"JOHN, WHAT THE SHIT? OH MY GOD!" my cousin Stephanie yelled from a distant hole. My cousins and aunt and uncle had seen the whole thing.

"HOLY FACK," my cousin Nikki yelled. "I HOPE SHE'S OKAY!"

I was embarrassed and just wanted the audience to go away.

My aunt Judy was a little softer with her approach. "Maybe let Jill drive," she chuckled.

"I didn't mean to!" I yelled as Jill got back in the cart. I rubbed her arm, kissed her, and apologized profusely. "Honey, I am sooo sorry. Are you okay?"

She seemed shaken up, but not too badly. "I could've twisted my ankle," she said.

Greg and Scotty drove by, both of their mouths open in the biggest shocked smiles you've ever seen. The three of us exchanged mischievous, silent giggles without Jill seeing and drove on to the next hole. I'm glad they had my back. I couldn't take one more person pointing out the obvious to me, which was that this couldn't happen ever again.

I had to protect this woman at all costs for she didn't slow me down one bit, which was obviously a lifesaver. My dad would've been beyond smitten with her after that day and most likely offered to pay for the entire wedding if I had proposed before the end of the weekend. And that golf tournament was his kind of day. Laughter, sunshine, and five hours playing his favorite sport on earth.

It made me proud of how far I'd come since that first year of grieving. Yes there was some sadness, but there was three times as much joy.

It's worth noting Jill hasn't played golf with me since.

STAGE 5: FINDING COMFORT IN ALL THE WEIRD PLACES

This is when you start talking to anyone or anything that'll listen.

CHAPTER 16
DAD'S APPARENTLY A BIRD NOW

I'VE HEARD it said that people can take on the form of an animal after they pass away. Do I have any scientific backing to support that claim? No. But every time Sami sees a bird, squirrel, or other small creature that is often seen in a New England backyard, she swears it's you-know-who.

"There was a blue jay just staring at me as I was doing dishes. I'm telling you, it's Dad!" she blurted out while we were all having coffee in Nantucket once.

"Was it sarcastic?" I deadpanned.

"No, but I had just been talking to Todd about Dad and how I wished I could ask him a question, and then suddenly I looked up and this big blue jay was perched on a branch just outside my kitchen window."

"So it had to be him." Sarah chuckled.

Sami saw the humor in it, but she did genuinely believe Dad was that bird. She made quite a case to back it up. By five p.m. I was convinced. Then weeks later, she swore he was a squirrel, and it threw all her credibility out the window, nearly hitting my bird/squirrel father in the process.

I want to believe that this wacky theory is true. I really do. I want to believe that my father, whom I lost so many years ago, shows himself in the unlikeliest of forms. Like a dumb chipmunk. I think when someone you love has died, you also just want that person around so much you'll imagine them in a way that is convenient and also impossible to prove wrong.

My great-aunt Helen came back as a cat.

How do you know?

How do you know it's NOT true? Not like we can cross-examine the cat.

Point taken.

My dad was an ambitious person, so the fact that between me and my sisters we've seen him take on the shape of probably eight different species kind of holds up. He's had a weird path, though, since his death, as far as his progression of animals is concerned. Like most old people he just shrinks and shrinks over the years, even as a shape-shifting animal.

After he first passed I swore he was in the body of Tucket, our family's yellow lab. Tucket would look at me both lovingly and also impatiently like, "Did you fix the shower door yet?," so it had to be my father.

Sami has seen him as both a bird and a squirrel. That's when I noticed the downgrade on the animals he was choosing to shack up in. At Sarah's wedding, he was either a seal or a butterfly. Tough to tell. During the ceremony, while the rest of the wedding party and I stood on a bluff overlooking Tom

Nevers Beach in Nantucket, a handful of butterflies swooped in gracefully and proceeded to hang out on Sarah's veil. They took turns opening and closing their wings.

Suddenly there were about five butterflies on the back of my sister's veil. They took turns slowly opening and closing their wings. It was insane and magnificent. It sounds cheesy, but it was a moment of "Dad? Is that you?!"

People began to point to the ocean in excitement. I figured maybe they thought the birds in the water were shark fins, a rookie mistake. That's when I saw six seals all lined up in the ocean staring at us. HOW IS THAT POSSIBLE? Before this I'd only ever seen one or two at a time maximum.

So, friends of the jury, what is your verdict? Was my dad a seal or a butterfly that day? Can he be both? Were the other animals my dead relatives? Is being a seal cooler because you can explore underwater? And do circus tricks? Or maybe it's being a butterfly, since people are always happy to see you and don't scream because they think you're a shark.

I really can't say with confidence which I think he was that day. Here's why.

Many times on Tom Nevers Beach, I've seen a seal's head pop up in the water like fifty feet away. It always scares the shit out of me even though I've been told they don't mean any harm, *but* that could be my dad, especially since he liked to swim and our relationship was based on him wanting to hang out with me even when I didn't want to hang out with him. (At least until college. Before then it was a lot of him wanting to be productive and me being a lazy teenager.)

Now for the butterfly theory. Obviously there was the sudden showing of a bunch of them at Sarah's wedding, which is very rare. Sure, you see one once in a while. Maybe two if you're in the countryside or in a Countryside Lemonade commercial. But five? That can't be Mother Nature randomly charming us with her presence. It has to be deeper than that. Like when I saw them in LA.

In our last year in LA, Jill and I moved to the less desirable part of Culver City. We didn't know it would be our last year out west, but we knew it was only a matter of time. Plus our new neighbors loved to blast mariachi music, so the countdown to our departure was slowly ticking whether we realized or not. On weekend nights it sucked living there due to the noise, but during a weekday when I'd be home because I was in between freelance gigs, it was magical.

I'd take breaks from writing to throw the ball for our dog, Koji, in the driveway, an activity that never got old for her. Something interesting would always happen on those quiet, calm weekdays at the bungalow—the appearance of butterflies. Sometimes it was just one. Other times it was two. But every time I saw one, it instantly relaxed me and put a smile on my face. Seeing them always made me think of my dad. Maybe because it always happened on days I was working on this book, so obviously I was thinking of him.

I like to think that he appears to remind me that life is short. I get cranky quite often. I'm the opposite of that cliché phrase: I *do* sweat the small stuff. And I often see what I don't have versus what I do. But seeing a butterfly that could or could not have been my dad always, at least in LA, made me smile. It always snapped me out of whatever was stirring in my head at the time and made me realize, "You're playing fetch at two on a Tuesday. How bad can life be?"

And maybe that's what it's like for Sami as well. When she sees a bird, a squirrel, or a rabbit that has two chins, it reminds her of our dad because it looks like him or because at that moment she was thinking of him. It's her nice reminder to practice appreciation, not wallow in depression.

Maybe it's as crazy as it sounds. Or maybe it's super simple. Jack Colbert is a renaissance man as far as heaven is concerned. He can do whatever the hell he wants. Today he's a puppy. Tomorrow he's a dragonfly. No matter what, he's still my dad. And, oh yeah, he's dead, so we can pretend he's whatever we want.

CHAPTER 17
EAT, PRAY, CRY

IF YOU SAVE up 256,000 airline miles using a Chase Sapphire Preferred card, you can fly round trip to Bali for free to see your dad's spirit on your honeymoon. You'll even have enough points to bring your partner too. I know this because that's what happened when Jill and I went in 2018 for our honeymoon. I also know that 'Bali Belly' is real, and even though that trip was beyond incredible, the three days of diarrhea I experienced when we got back were not. But before there was me, weak on the couch, living off saltines and bone broth, there was vacation me, getting ready to visit a spiritual healer in the jungle town of Ubud.

What do you wear to see a spiritual healer? A blazer and dark jeans like it's a client presentation? Gym attire so you're comfy? Do healers even have a dress code? Do they participate in casual Fridays? So many questions, so little time.

"We should head to the front desk," I said as I adjusted my khaki shorts and Nantucket tee and Nike Air Max 90s. Basically what I wear whether I'm in the northeast suburbs or Southeast Asia. "We're gonna be late!"

"Coming!" Jill said. She exited the bathroom and flew past me, out the hotel room door, proving what my dead dad would have said about her never slowing me down. Seconds later we were power-walking down the narrow, stone paths that snaked throughout the entire boutique hotel property. As we made our way around the pool and entered the lobby, I spotted our driver waiting patiently, leaning against his car. I also spotted his fanny pack, which he wore proudly. It was black, made of faux leather, and gave off a vibe I was into. I glanced over at the front desk. Two women stood behind it with military-grade posture and angel-approved warmness. They bowed immediately while smiling.

"Hi, how are youuuuuu?" they asked in unison.

"Good, thank you," I replied because I'm surprisingly pleasant when I'm on vacation.

Healers in Bali are like therapists in LA: everyone knows of a good one. But Jill gets credit for this specific request; seeing a healer had been on her trip wish list ever since we booked our 'Bali Moon.' The hotel staff suggested we see Made Lunas. The name sounds *made* up (I hate myself for that pun, don't worry), but it's pretty standard in those parts. 'Made' is the name given to every second-born male in Bali, and for the record, it's pronounced *ma-day*. The hotel suggested we go on a Monday since it was during a full moon cycle.

There we sat in the back of our driver's car as it coursed its way past rice paddies and barefoot moped drivers. Our driver, like most in Bali, had a small Mitsubishi SUV. It's like that's where all those cars went in the late nineties when America lost interest. And, like most of the drivers there, he was cheap and on Instagram.

Ten minutes later we arrived at our destination. Made Lunas's home was traditional Balinese, a compound surrounded by walls of whitewashed mud and brick with little pavilions serving as the bedrooms, living areas, and kitchen, with small, open courtyards in between. Like most traditional houses in Indonesia, spatial orientation and hierarchy are taken into consideration. It's based on a Hindu dharma principle that states that every object in the universe is conceived as having an ideal location. If this is aligned well, then harmony within the universe can be achieved, basically allowing its residents to achieve a perfect state of being. Pretty sweet, right? It's also common for extended family to live within the compound as well. If I did this, my in-laws would need their own TV for MSNBC and I'd need my own bar.

As we entered the compound, it felt extremely similar to the movie *Eat, Pray, Love*– specifically the scene where Julia Roberts sees a healer, not the one where she bangs Javier Bardem. Made's wife greeted us and encouraged us to put on sarongs, thereby answering my dress-code question, and wait in the small pavilion that looked like a living room. It was about ten-by-ten with a thin, hand-woven rug on the floor and Hindu decorations on shelves.

Jill and I smiled at one another, full of excitement. This had been her idea, but I was equally psyched. As a writer you are often complaining because you can easily point out the problems in a less-than-ideal situation, but on the flipside, if something sucks, you've got good material. Speaking of which, we were feeling all special and adventurous because no one back home could claim they had seen a healer in Bali.

But then Made's pavilion door opened and our doppel-gangers stepped out. Sure, she was a blonde and there's no way he was as charming as me, but basically we realized couples seeing healers on their honeymoon were a dime a dozen. But fuck it. We were anxious people, we wanted to be "healed," and our friends and family still considered us "cool" to our faces, so that was all that mattered. Right?!

We were still amused at our lack of originality when we saw Made himself standing in the doorway. It was dark except for a window on the far wall, which backlit his silhouette. He gave us the courteous head bow and smile, cueing us to stand up and join him, but as we did he suddenly held up his hand, gesturing for us to wait. Uh-oh. My legs and hips now felt broken from sitting cross-legged for not even two minutes, so I awkwardly tried to descend back down toward the floor. I collapsed in doing so.

His wife came over. "He just needs a moment," she explained. "Then he will be with you shortly. Thank youuuu."

She wasn't kidding. A moment later Made gave us the signal to proceed. I climbed the stairs behind Jill, up to Made Lunas's sanctuary. At five-foot-six with bare feet planted in a duckfooted stance, Made was like a Balinese Bob Hoskins from *Hook*. I noticed he was wearing a linen cap, a white linen button-down, and loose-fitting dark khaki pants that stopped before his ankles. Like Bali capris? Is that a thing? Who knows. This was my first rodeo.

He bowed; we bowed back. "Please." He gestured toward the floor.

Jill and I sat down next to each other and crossed our legs again. Hers was graceful. Mine involved a grunt or two. I glanced over and watched Made as he lit a candle, then said a quick prayer in front of his Hindu shrine. He was either preparing to heal us or merely tolerate us. Either would be an impressive accomplishment. It goes without saying that I'm no aficionado when it comes to healing, but man, did this feel authentic! Way cooler than the psychic we saw in LA that lived above an auto body shop! (That's a true story for another time).

Made then quietly and gracefully sat down to my left, perpendicular to Jill and me so he could see us both. "What brings you to Bali?" he asked with a warm, old-mannish smile. While we took turns answering his question, we each watched with curiosity as he began breaking up little sticks into the length of matches. He laid them on the ground to his right in some sort of pattern. One would be horizontal, the next would be vertical. While we chatted, pausing slightly at times, wondering what the hell he was doing and exchanging subtle but confused expressions, he built on the wooden floor some sort of design with the sticks. Content with his little arts and crafts project, he regained his yoga-teacher-pose and spoke.

"First I will start with her because she is the boss."

Jill and I chuckled even if he does use that joke for every coed couple.

"You are fire," he said. Then to me, "He is water." He paused, smiled at us, and continued with his revelation. "You cannot make coffee with just water. And you cannot make it with just fire. You need both to make coffee. Working together."

The metaphor made sense, and I do love coffee. But anyone who knows my wife and I knows that I'm *fire*—passionate, ambitious, fidgety, and annoying–whereas Jill is *water*–calm, grounded, physically strong, and pees a lot. Actually, I pee more.

I want to relay all of the wisdom, guidance, and comfort Made laid down on Jill during our session, I really do, but I can't remember a lick of it. Neither can she. I know because I'm texting her as I write this. What I can recall is what Made said once he finally turned to me because I wrote it down the second we got back to our hotel. When Made finished healing Jill, he recomposed himself by closing his eyes and taking a deep breath. After a moment he rotated at the torso while slowly opening his eyes like the Terminator. I immediately tooted.

"Tell me about your family," he said. "Do you have any brothers or sisters?"

"Yes. I have two older sisters and one younger sister."

"Parents? Are they both alive?"

"My mother is, but my father passed away."

He nodded, then gestured toward the floor.

"Let me show you. Your mother." He gestured to the solo stick at the top of the stick pyramid, which was turned horizontally. His hand rotated so it was palm up, and like Vanna White, he waved it over toward the next stick. This one, below my mother, was in the same horizontal position.

"Sister..." His hand continued toward the next stick, which was horizontal below it, and he said "sister" again. His hand floated over the third stick that was below Pookie; this one was now vertical. "Boy is like this." He pointed down toward his own crotch. "Because you see–" His hand modeling went from PG to

NC-17 as he made a fist in front of his crotch and stuck out just his index finger. "The stick like that represents man." He pointed to me with his hand-puppet-penis. He laughed, and so did I. I felt healed already. "And then sister," he continued, showing the stick below mine was horizonal like the other Colbert women.

I let out an unfiltered "whoa!" He had laid all this out before he knew anything about us. Obviously I was impressed but naturally skeptical. I don't know if the hotel gave Made our real names and he was able to cheat and do his homework before we arrived, like comb our social media profiles or break into our hotel room and find out our deepest, darkest secrets from one strand of hair his team found on Jill's hairbrush like they do on *CSI*. Regardless, I was loving every minute of it. There is a benefit to alternative modes of medicine even if they are unproven. There was no TV on, no texts or emails coming in, not a care in the world. The peacefulness of it all was therapeutic enough. Which is why I sat there, patiently waiting for more zen to flow in, when Made suddenly got quiet and began looking me up and down. My awkward, no-teeth smile appeared as a natural reflex.

"You have pain in your back?"

"Yeah," I admitted, "in my lower back."

"Okay, I will take that away."

Seriously? Thank god.

"Do you have any questions for me?"

"Yes. I want to know about my career. I feel like I'm not living up to my potential and doing what I'm passionate about. I'm tired of always having to do stuff on the side to get closer to my dreams."

"Hm." He closed his eyes. "You will always be doing something on the side. No matter what."

I closed my eyes, too, and just let the depression wash over me. Crap.

"You try and do too many things at once. Just pick one. You need to work for her."

He and I both looked at Jill, who flashed a giddy smile. I couldn't tell if he meant like work so my income benefits her or work with Jill so she was my boss. Jill obviously took it as the latter.

I chimed in. "We're thinking of moving back east. Any guidance on that?"

"You will own a home in under nine years." He said it like he was content with that answer.

"Nine years?!" Jill barked.

I made a face as I turned to her. She was looking off into the distance, clearly calculating a positive spin on this news. Most interior designers want a home they can make amazing ASAP. Jill was no different and not afraid to pick up a drill and do beautiful damage no matter where we lived. She would've put a deck on the bungalow we rented in Culver City if I didn't remind her fifty times that we were just renting. When I turned back to Made he was still staring at me, which naturally caught me off guard. But I was quickly learning that his biggest plot points were always delivered this way. I was curious what was next.

That's when he hit me with a bomb.

"Your father is here. In fact he was here before we started. He's sitting just a few feet behind you."

I'm sorry, can you repeat that? I wanted to say. *It sounds like you said my dad was here.* But I didn't say any of this out loud. Instead my eyelids began to twitch. Apparently ever since I entered Made's little hut, there had been an emotional storm on the horizon. That's why every cell in my body began to batten down the hatches. We were about to get torn apart, y'all! Made, unaware of the fun panic attack I was having, continued.

"That's why I told you to wait outside before coming in. I was busy talking to him. He has so much he wants to tell you." Made was now smiling, happy to finally tell me this news.

I was doing the opposite as I began ugly crying. The tear ducts were open and unleashing a fury down my face. I couldn't control it. It was unreal. And guess what? Turns out there is a proper wardrobe for a spiritual healer when you've lost a loved one in the past. It's called a Gore-Tex onesie. I needed all the waterproof protection I could get, for tears were raining down my face with no signs of slowing down. Which Made, because he's some Balinese wizard, saw coming.

"I started with her first because your father said you'd be crying the whole time if we started with you and we'd never get to her!"

Jill and I both laughed, which gave my eyes a ten-second break from grieving.

"He's trying to keep his distance as we speak because he knows the closer he gets to you, the more emotional you'll feel."

He suddenly shot his arm up as if to tell someone "hold on!," then turned back to me. "He wants to say so much!" Made said, both agitated and amused. He looked out of the corner of his eye toward the empty corner of the room and nodded in agreement. "Your father is persistent. But he just keeps staring at you and smiling. Like he's enamored by you."

At this point I was no longer crying. I was blubbering. It was such a small, intimate space with just the three of us, and I had fully lost control. If I ever start to cry, it's always related to me thinking about my dad. It might happen on a public bus, but I can keep it contained. I can keep the tears in their respective lane and under control. This was the opposite. There was no lane; there were no bright orange cones or guardrails. The tears were flowing down my face, and I kept trying to wipe them with my arms, which were sweaty thanks to the southeast Asian humidity. It was like trying to dry off after the shower with a wet towel.

"There are two other people standing off in the distance. A man and a woman. They look like your father."

I stopped crying. "That could be my grandparents, my dad's parents." That straightforward update gave me the breather I needed.

"Your father won't stop bugging me!" he laughed. "But he has five things he wants to tell you."

I had to look down. That's how intense this new round of crying was. That's when Jill's hand touched my knee to comfort me. *She never touches me enough, I thought to myself. I should do this more often!* While I was ready to never wash that knee again, Made leaned in and, using the fingers on his right hand, counted off the five pieces of advice, which were coming from apparently Jack Colbert himself.

"Keep love in the family. Your sisters, mother, communicate often."

I nodded.

"Keep love in your family! Your wife, children."

I nodded.

"Don't worry too much. Don't try and do so much to provide for your family. It'll be okay. Focus on one thing! You have all these ideas, and they're all good, but you can't do it all. Do one at a time and it'll be okay."

I smiled and, of course, nodded. My tears had finally stopped. I had it under control, so I could remember everything he was saying. Then he delivered what snipers like to call 'the kill shot.'

"He wants you to know that he didn't die of cancer."

Fuck, I give up. My body was now a Wet-Nap with legs.

"....he went because it was his time. God sent for him."

I'm not religious, but *sweet Jesus*, that touched me to the core. Honestly it felt like closure. It validated why Dad died so young, at the age of fifty-six. Made paused for dramatic effect before delivering the fifth and final message. He was good.

"He also says... I love you."

Up until now this entire healer session had been like sitting through an extraordinary five-course tasting menu dinner that takes all night; then, once all the plates have cleared and you're slowly working your way toward finishing the last few sips of wine, the chef comes out holding a doll-house-size plate with a dessert on it and you know it's something you'll never get a chance to eat ever again. As he formally places it on the table between you and your date, he says something to the effect of "I just wanted to say thank you for dining with me tonight. I make these at home; enjoy." My father's *I love you,* delivered via Made, was like that. A gesture that, while far-fetched, was easy to believe in my current state. And why not?

Made, bowed toward where my father, and, apparently,

grandparents were, as if touched by the experience and happy to have met them. Even if my dad was annoying the entire time.

"They are gone now," Made said as he began to recompose himself.

"Guess I just have to fly around the world to see him. Who knew?" I joked. Everyone in the room was thinking about making that joke. Only I was a big enough tool to say it. At this point Jill was probably thinking, *Great, glad no one showed up for me,* but both her parents are alive so she wins daily. As I blew my nose into a tissue that wished it had committed suicide back at the hotel and I sat up straight to fix my garbage posture, I started to notice Made scooting over toward me. He was suddenly facing me from about two feet away. I felt special, not gonna lie.

"I will take everything out, including the back pain. The stress. I will clear your body and mind of what needs clearing."

I braced myself. I needed this like yesterday.

In a series of breathwork movements, the healer inhaled and exhaled aggressively while keeping one palm on my chest. Both our eyes were closed while Jill was probably looking up cool sarongs on Etsy. Made breathed in through his nose and exhaled through his mouth. He gestured for me to do the same. It was like an eighties Lamaze class. Suddenly Made pushed his palm into my chest harder, said a series of Indonesian things that sounded cool, and did something like a karate move where he let out a grunt so deep and loud it shook some stuff out of my soul, and for a brief moment I worried about my underwear.

Our session with Made ended. He bowed, we bowed, all the spirits bowed. He gestured toward the doorway kindly, thanked us for letting him heal us, and smiled with kind eyes, which in American means "get the heck out." His next appointment, another damn white couple on their honeymoon, was up, and ours had run long thanks to my dad. As we walked down the steps into the courtyard, the bright sun hit my face, and I hissed like a vampire with an intolerance to sunlight. I felt exhausted. Grief is an invisible eight-hundred-pound gorilla. It's heavy and it drains you. Especially when you cry out fifteen gallons of water. This feeling of malaise, or pure weakness, reminded me of those last few months when my father was in and out of the ICU.

But this day was different. I truly felt connected to my father. It was interesting, it was funny, and it tickled the spiritual side of me. We checked a box on our Bali Moon that I'll never forget. Jill was validated in that she always knew she was the boss, but hearing a healer confirm it was priceless to her. And I got some equally priceless advice from my late father. While these things may seem bogus to most, I valued my session with Made greatly. When I get anxious about life or my lower back hurts, I go online and check out flights to Southeast Asia. I can get a deep tissue massage for a lot cheaper in Pennsylvania, but my dad's spirit clearly prefers a tropical climate.

Ghost problems, amiright?

STAGE 6: EMERGING VICTORIOUS AND DELIRIOUS

You're showering daily and able to show up to things on time.
What is happening?!

CHAPTER 18
HOLD THE LEG

WITH THE WOMAN who had become my wife five hours ago lying on the bed in her wedding dress, I leaned in and drunkenly said with a slight slur and a twinkle in my eye, "We should make a baby."

"Get a condom please," Jill said with much amusement. I had no idea that kids would come three years later. I also had no idea that becoming a dad would vastly make me miss my own.

But back in that hotel room the night of our wedding it makes you wonder: How does someone who is terrified to have kids suddenly propose trying to make one?

Happiness, that's how.

This is why it's better off that I don't have that much fun that often. I clearly don't know how to handle it. I was experiencing a high that started that day back in 2017 with sips of bourbon at noon with my groomsmen, then ended with late night pizza by the hotel bar with the last few night owls from our wedding. Our closest family and friends from Philadelphia,

Boston, and New York were forced to fly three thousand miles to celebrate our union in Long Beach, California. We even had a few friends from LA make the trek south. Everyone we loved was all in one place, something that'll never happen again until one of us is dead. Even then I'm sure we won't have as good of a turnout.

A year later that level of happiness returned, on our honeymoon in Bali, specifically at our second hotel, which was in Seminyak. We were enjoying our pasta dishes at an Italian joint when the topic of kids came up.

A smile grew on Jill's face. "I think I'm ready."

"I mean, we're not getting any younger!" I belted out in corny fashion.

Something magical was clearly happening on this honeymoon. Maybe it was just the power of a great vacation. Or maybe it was because I got to be with a ghost version of my dad earlier that week at the healer. Did he show up just to guide me to do the job he loved doing up until the day he passed? What, have sex? No, gross. I mean *being a father*.

Ten minutes later, as we got into our decadent suite brought to us by a fantastic currency exchange rate, we kicked off our shoes and crawled onto the bed. Jill leaned in, about to kiss me.

"Let's make a baby," she said with a fake slur.

"Damn it," I replied, "I was going to make that joke!"

→

. . .

My arms felt like they were going to snap off as I boarded the American Airlines plane in Philly. I had my son, Jack, in my right arm, his car seat in my left hand, my backpack on with half my apartment in it, and a duffel bag on my spare shoulder with kid's stuff in it. Someone needs to open a gym called 'Dads' where you use strollers as barbells and do supersets of flicking off light switches while turning thermostats down.

It was the first day of the Christmas holiday in 2021 and my mother had given to me... an all-inclusive trip to Saint Lucia, flop sweat, and a partridge in a pear tree. It was a very generous gift for my siblings and our families, one that was giving Jill and especially me anxiety as we were the only ones with two kids both under five flying internationally. It didn't help that two weeks prior, COVID was back in the US and on a tear.

Jill was behind me with our daughter, Jane, in her arms, who was not even four months old at the time. As I looked up, Jill locked eyes with me above her mask. It looked like she had seen some shit, but now that we were on plane, a lot of relief was slowly lifting the burden off our shoulders. This burden was both figurative and literal as I put Jack in the middle seat of our row so I could buckle in his car seat at the window. Once we were all settled in, I felt like I couldn't relax or something bad would happen. Could I sleep? Yeah, right. I looked to my left. Jill was breastfeeding Jane. I looked to the window seat. My son had his eyes closed with headphones on and an iPad in his lap, calmly eating apple slices.

He looked like he was at a Sandals resort.

Jill and I looked like we had just escaped Cuba.

·   ·   ·

⇀

When Jill was twelve weeks pregnant with our first child, we got the exciting news that we were having a boy. I would've happily taken either, but I had a boy name in the arsenal just waiting to be used. One my sisters had reserved for me to claim. One you can easily guess at this point in my story.

It was a 'two birds, one stone' situation because not only was it in honor of my father, but Jill's grandfather as well—a man who had coincidentally passed away when my father-in-law was young. By naming our son Jack, we'd be honoring two great men with one simple name. Almost everyone loved this idea, though some needed some time to let it sink in. By some, I mean Sarah.

"Wait, I didn't know that's what you're naming him," Sarah said, visibly upset when we told her. To be clear, she wasn't mad, just very emotional. We were in Boston with my family for Easter weekend when Jill was about four months pregnant. The conversation during Easter lunch had been all things baby. We had been telling tons of family recently from both sides, but we had never sent out an official telegram with the big update. Guess we should've, huh?

"Sarah, what's the big deal? I thought you knew," I said.

"Clearly I didn't," she replied through tears.

That's the problem with constantly paying tribute to your dead dad's legacy. Shit gets emotional. I always knew if I had a son I'd name him Jack. There was never any hesitation about it.

. . .

The only hesitation I had was when it came to the prep. I tried to read all the books; I really did. But the words on the page would go in my brain and right back out of it. I tried to compensate by not being difficult with any of the in-person stuff.

"Would you rather we do a birth class that is like two hours long, one night a week for six weeks, or a seven-hour course on a Saturday?" Jill asked one night a few weeks later.

"Let's just get the torture done all in one day," I replied.

We found ourselves at the Bok Building in South Philly on a balmy July. The class started with us watching a video where a brave woman, with the help of her doula and husband, did a home birth. Ten super-pregnant women sat around, bobbing up and down on exercise balls, while their husbands sat beside them on wooden chairs, holding their snacks and water with facial expressions like they were watching D-Day footage. That is to say, pure fear and a little confusion. We all watched in the dark as the woman in the video did a series of poses and physical movements throughout her house to help her work through the contractions that riddled her body. Then, for the finale, I found my eyes widening as I watched this woman defy anything I've ever seen in the movies. She gave birth while standing, bent over a chair for support. The little guy gently slid out of her lady region with the assistance of the doula. The husband cried, the wife cried, and the doula held the baby in a swaddle like it was a fresh loaf of French bread. The lights turned on.

The chipper instructor, who was bobbing on an exercise ball at the head of the class, looked at all of us bright-eyed and with more energy than a kid in a GoGurt commercial.

"That was a home birth with a doula. Any questions? Was that what you expected or not?"

I looked around the room. Everyone looked shaken. I had so many questions.

"Um, yeah, just one," I said. "Or more like an observation. I had no idea you could give birth like that! Like, aren't legs supposed to be up in stirrups and ten people standing around helping?"

Everyone laughed. Easy audience. Instant ego boost.

"Seriously! What's a doula?" a husband asked.

The instructor laughed.

Everyone started to loosen up and not filter with their questions or comments. What was interesting was seeing it all from the dads' perspectives. What I didn't realize was the men could be just as tense and nervous as their wives. The wives had the terror of their first birth looming ahead, whereas the men had the terror of triggering their wives because they weren't present during the class or clueless when the delivery day did arrive.

I was exiting the bathroom just as another husband was exiting the class for his own bathroom break. He glanced behind him, then forward again to make sure we were the only two souls in the massive hallway. He opened his mouth like he was going to ask me something personal or confide in me. Instead he burped so loudly and aggressively I wasn't just surprised, I was impressed. He also rotated his head in a circular motion as he blew the remainder out to make sure none of it hit me head on. That's what we call 'manners.'

"Oh god, I've been waiting since we started to do that," he said.

"Pregnancy is hard on both partners; I get it," I said.

We both laughed. It seemed like us future dads were all in the trenches together and this new life stage would make it easier for me to make new guy friends.

I was excited.

→

After a five-hour flight, then a two-hour van ride from the airport, we arrived at our resort in Saint Lucia: The Landings. It was a very nice, all-inclusive hotel right on the water. My entire family was with us. Except for our grand matriarch.

Due to COVID protocols, there was a Verifly app we all had to download the week prior to our vacation, onto which we had to upload nine hundred forms proving we had a clean bill of health. When my mother showed up to the airport that morning in Boston she didn't have her Verifly app all filled out and confirmed, so Delta wouldn't let her board. She had to spend the night at an airport hotel. Apparently she got a grilled cheese from room service and watched TV.

Fortunately the travel agent was able to help her get everything squared away and on the first flight out the next morning. In the meantime we settled into our beautiful two-bedroom suite. As did Natalie.

"Ohh, baby cakes!" she yelled from the other room.

Did I mention we were sharing the suite with my mom and sister? It had been an extremely long day. We were exhausted. Jill had set up Jack's crib in the kitchen with a blackout tent on top. She was setting up Jane's crib in our closet at the moment.

It felt like this might actually all work out.

"John?" Jill asked.

I went into our bedroom.

"We forgot diapers for Jane."

Of course we did.

→

Words can't describe the feeling of seeing your child being delivered right before your eyes. You have seen ultrasounds of this little thing in your wife's womb, but it isn't 4D. There's no portrait mode on the machine to make the background out of focus and the baby picture clear so you can see their exact features. So when they do emerge for the first time, the reveal can be overwhelming and emotional. And for the mother? It's of course insanely physical.

It didn't help that Jack's birth was anything but seamless. Jill had back labor for close to forty-eight hours. We made multiple trips to the hospital with Jill reeling in pain only to be told the same thing every time and sent home: "You're not dilated enough to be admitted."

Back to our apartment we'd go. Every two hours I woke up to Jill either wide awake in bed or wide awake, soaking in a bath. In either location she was reeling in excruciating pain. I'd fetch Tylenol, snacks, and try to push on her tailbone to relieve the pain like the birthing coach had taught us, but it felt like I was putting a *Finding Dory* Band-Aid on a gunshot wound. Me and my methods felt useless, like a husband in a housewares commercial trying to put the entire oven into the dishwasher like an idiot.

Turns out 'third time's a charm.' When we arrived at the hospital the third day, Jill was finally asked the question she had waited two days and two nights to hear.

"Would you like an epidural?" the doctor asked. Jill could now be admitted and better yet–given beautiful modern medicine.

Jill nodded her head so aggressively I thought she was going to break her neck. Thirty minutes later she was licking a Popsicle and giggling. She even laughed at one of my jokes. Clearly the epidural can make all sorts of painful things feel pleasant.

→

"Is Pookie back from the bar yet?" I asked Jill.

"I don't know."

We had just put our kids down for the night. I stepped out onto the suite's balcony and looked toward the bar at the restaurant.

"Crap, she's still down there."

I was happy that my mother had finally arrived in Saint Lucia after being stuck in Boston for twenty-four hours, but now that she was here I wanted her to get back here in our suite so she could be our sitter. You don't realize how effortless so many things are until you have kids and it's not effortless anymore. Like stepping out, period. Pookie's babysitting gig here on the island was easy, but we still knew the full value it was offering us. It helped that the kids were asleep. All Pookie had to do was sit with the monitors. Key word being 'with the monitors.' Right now she was 'with the DJ.'

I went into the bathroom to brush my teeth as Jill changed her outfit. "Hopefully she comes back soon."

Suddenly the door opened and we heard what sounded like a trucker clear his throat a few times. Eventually she 'got it.' We all cringed.

"Ugh," Pookie said.

"Gross," Natalie said. She was on her bed on her phone as Mom took her shoes off in the entryway.

"Natalie, that's rude," Pookie snapped.

I came out of our room. "Mom, you okay to still watch the monitors for us?"

"You guys don't wanna just hang here?" she asked.

We both looked at Jill, who for the first time in a while, was wearing both lipstick and earrings. I had pants on. Of course we didn't.

Read the room, Pookie.

→

Being in a hospital while your kid is close to being born is an adrenaline rush. Different than anything else I've experienced. At one point I stepped out to get some air, but when I returned to Jill's delivery room, her nurse, Allison, was in full-on beast mode.

"Dad, why don't you sit over here? We're going to start pushing harder now so we can get this baby out!" She was intent on getting our baby out before her shift ended at midnight.

Jill was in the position with her feet in the stirrups and was suddenly pushing as hard as she could. The room now felt forty degrees warmer than a second ago. Crap, was I getting light-headed? Nurse Allison saw some of the color drain from my face.

"You're not gonna be one of those guys that passes out, are you?" she asked.

I swallowed a teaspoon's worth of throw-up that had silently crept up my throat before responding, "Definitely not!" That was all the pep talk I needed.

"Good," she said as she came over and grabbed Jill's left leg and hoisted it up to act as a stirrup. She made eye contact with me, practically looking through my soul like we were about to storm the beaches of Normandy. "Grab a leg."

When Nurse Allison says grab a leg, you grab a goddamn leg. I picked Jill's right leg up under her knee and stood there, bracing myself for Crazy Town. That's when Dr. Ufberg, Jill's primary doctor, entered the room. It was amazing that he was available during our pregnancy. Usually, it's like the scene in *Knocked Up*; you don't always get your doctor when you deliver. We had lucked out, and we were psyched to get ours. He grabbed a stool on wheels and slid over, smiling, like he was about to check the oil on a '57 Chevy.

"All right, Mom, we ready to do this?" he asked but didn't need an answer. He then said some medical things to everyone in the room, and nurses and techs rushed to their positions in perfect harmony, without knocking into each other once.

Suddenly we heard a blood-curdling scream from next door.

A random nurse monitoring one of the machines looked at us. "Natural birth."

Jill and I exchanged looks. We then decided it might be best to play some music to drown out the 'Natural Birthing Sounds' playlist that was blasting next door. I grabbed my phone and put on Spotify. Ironically "Slide Away" by Miley Cyrus came on.

"Push, Jill, push!" Dr. Ufberg said.

She listened.

After twenty minutes he perked up. "Does Dad wanna come see the head?" He was excited.

Dad was not. Dad was about to hurl. I leaned over to look way down into the darkness in what a normal person would refer to as Jill's crotch. I could see the very top of Jack's darkly-haired head. It looked like a baseball covered in hair. Yup, the room was now 400 degrees.

"Wow," I said in monotone, like someone who is terrified of roller coasters trying to sound excited as the roller coaster climbs to the top of the first hill. I resumed my position by Jill's side and felt a bead of sweat run down my forehead and into my eye like GET ME OUT OF HERE. I looked up. Nurse Allison was staring at me, waiting for me to puke, poop, or pass out. I distracted myself by finding the time on my phone.

11:45 p.m.

I leaned over to Jill. "If you can hold out, he won't be born on 9/11," I joked.

She laughed, too, in between extreme rounds of pushing, but apparently she didn't take the request seriously. She pushed like a champ, and every time Ufberg challenged her to dig deep and push harder, the competitive side in Jill triumphed. As Miley Cyrus serenaded us into parenthood at 11:53 p.m., our little prince emerged from Jill's vag and officially took the stage. I'm going to tell you right now that all the cliché things parents, especially dads, tell you about birthing stories are true. When that baby does come out, it's mind-blowing. My entire body was flooded with emotions, and I had to hold back from suddenly exploding into tears. I had bouts of fear that something might happen to Jill during the birth because of all the scary pain she had been in for forty-eight hours prior–plus, I've seen a lot of movies–so that sense of relief, combined with finally seeing our son for the very first time, was overwhelming. He was covered in blood and had so much hair on his head he looked like a forty-year-old man. An almost nine-pound middle-aged man. It was insane.

When Jill and I found out she was pregnant Sami found a letter my father had written to my mother after I was born. After two girls, the day I was born he got a son. The letter read as follows:

Dear Cheryl,

Now our family truly is complete!

Love,

Jack

My sisters don't love that letter, which I can understand, but it makes me happy. Now my Jack was here, and I was in love.

. . .

→

The Vista V2 stroller from UPPABaby is crafted with premium textiles and leather accents. Ironically as I pulled it across the hot, thick Caribbean sand, none of that shit mattered.

Here's a free tip: Maybe don't bring a full-size stroller to the beach.

People were staring as I dragged it to our spot twenty-five yards down the sand. We had brought this freakin' behemoth since Jane was a newborn and Jack was two, and the resort was very spread out. Plus, Jane could nap in it, which she was about to do. I pulled the stroller behind a chair so it was under the shade of an umbrella. Jill came over and put Jane in. She passed out immediately.

"Jack, do you wanna go for a swim with Daddy?" I asked my son.

"I don't want to!" Jack snapped. I looked over to see him morphing into some little Satan child. The terrible twos aren't some old wives' tale. We had been in Saint Lucia for three days now and Jack still hadn't gone in the water. Mind you, we thought this would be great for Jack, the ocean being a beautiful, calm bath down in the Caribbean. The water was an incredible mix of green and blue, like a nineties screensaver. Little kids were walking, splashing, and bonding with their parents as I looked around. I wanted that.

"Time for the tough-love approach," I said as I marched towards Jack and picked him up. *He's gonna love the water,* I thought; *he's just so defiant. He hated baths at first, and now he loves them. This will be the same.*

We made it ten feet before his forty-pound body was bucking in my arms so hard I had to put him down.

I think I pulled something in my neck.

—→

If Jack's birth was a climb up Everest for Jill, Jane's was a sled ride down it.

As a hurricane tore through the city of Philadelphia, Jill began to push at the same hospital where Jack was born. There was no back labor. No baths being drawn at three a.m. to help Jill's pain because she couldn't sleep. The only thing familiar this time around was the company.

"NURSE ALLISON?!" I yelled.

Allison looked up as she entered the room, scared.

"Yes, I'm Allison."

Turns out the same nurse that delivered Jack would help deliver Jane.

"You helped deliver our son, Jack!" I said, excited.

"Oh, cool," she said.

Turns out not all of us were excited about this fact.

Within the hour, Jane practically fell out of Jill. She was in labor for a total of six hours. About forty-two less than with Jack.

Jane was bigger at nine point three pounds, yet beautiful. With Jill's full lips, my blue eyes and reddish hair, she was a cutie. To be honest I had wanted a girl from the get-go. I grew up with all women, and I've never felt that I'm the most masculine of men. I don't watch sports, I'm a fan of Bravo, and I think Amy Schumer is funny. I was nervous I wouldn't be able to teach a son how to be a strong man. Turns out that was all bull-shit. Plus, there's YouTube.

With Jane, meanwhile, I could teach her to not take any shit from lame men. To be a firecracker with high standards and a quick wit. I'd be Obi Wan, and she'd be Luke.

She'd be Daddy's little girl.

I'd be screwed.

→

The only thing that can take the air out of a tropical trip during the holidays with your immediate family is strong COVID protocols.

We were in the nurses' station at The Landings Resort. Our flight was leaving in eight hours. We all did COVID kit tests in our hotel rooms, but Jack had to get one in person since he was under five years old.

If he tested positive, we couldn't board the plane later.

If the airline didn't get the test results by two p.m., we couldn't board the plane.

If the nurse stayed on 'island time,' we'd be here for a month.

"Okay, all set," the nurse said as she finished the swab in Jack's nose. She sealed it up to be sent to the lab.

We stood there. We were going to need way more assur-ance than that.

"Soooo... our flight leaves at two p.m. This will definitely get tested in time for that, right?" Jill asked with a level of calm that surprised me.

"Yes, yes," the nurse assured us with a smile.

We weren't buying it.

"Okay, thanks!" I said, and then, unconvinced, we went back to our room to pack.

Two hours later, we all piled into two vans to head to the airport.

Still no test results.

On the windy road we went, chatting about what a beautiful trip it was. Jane was falling asleep in her car seat. Jack was content, looking out the window. The scenery was lovely as the road curled around a mountain overlooking the harbor. The palm trees were boldly green. Locals smiled and waved at our van as we passed. As the van powered forward, winding around the turns, accelerating up hills, and slamming on the brakes at every stop sign.

Not a light braking to a stop.

A slam.

I watched from the very back as our torsos swayed from side to side due to the windy road and the driver's not so great driving. I realized I was getting carsick, and I wasn't alone.

"I think I'm getting nauseous."

Jill turned to look at me. I could tell from her pale face she was feeling the same way. Oh god.

"Sarah, can you open the window next to you? I need some air."

"Ugh, yeah," Sarah replied like she was fighting off some puke too.

Pookie fanned herself.

We were all slowly headed for Throw-Up Town. Except one.

"Are mopeds much more economical here?" Jonathan asked. He was riding shotgun. Much like first class seats are above the nose on international flights so there's zero turbulence, Jonathan was having a grand old time up front. His body wasn't rocking side to side like he was on a sailboat fighting forty-foot waves. This made him happy as a clam and chatty as fuck.

I took my attention off the front and looked outside trying to distract myself from getting even more sick. At least we had a negative COVID test from Jack.

Oh wait, no, we didn't.

The vans pulled up to the Saint Lucia airport two hours later. We burst out into the fresh air like animals let loose from a zoo.

"OH MY GOD," I let out.

One by one we huffed the air, thankful not one of us had ralphed. Jill was bent over trying to get her bearings.

"What's wrong with everyone?" Jonathan asked, oblivious.

We shot him a group death stare, sending him scurrying to the back of the van to see if the driver needed help unloading our bags.

We ended up enduring what was the most stressful forty-five minutes of my life in that ticket line. I kept pacing and making sure Jack didn't run away while the incredible American Airlines agents called our hotel and the lab that Jack's sample was sent to, nonstop, to get the results so we could get our boarding passes. At one point Jill had to breastfeed Jane while we stood there because we couldn't stray far from the ticket desk in the tiny island airport. My family felt awful, but they had to go to the gate. I almost broke down in tears. I thought we were going to be spending the night at some dingy hotel with zero kid supplies and zero extended family to help.

"He tested negative," one of the agents finally said.

Jill almost spiked Jane like she just scored a touchdown.

→

Jill does this great trick where she will sign cards on behalf of our kids. Even for our furry ones.

"Happy Birthday! Love, Koji," I read out loud one year. Koji, our dog, had gotten me a card. There was even a paw print. I was touched.

On my first Father's Day, I opened the card to read the nice, generic message printed inside. Below it, though, read:

Love ya, Dada, Jack.

I teared up. Obviously at nine months old Jack didn't hold a pen and sign his name in cursive. I was emotional because the torch had officially been passed. I was no longer just a son.

I was a dad too.

Father's Day would no longer be sad to me. It would no longer be a day I dreaded and had to emotionally prepare for. It was no longer a day to mourn. It was a day to celebrate as well. Now as a dad I miss mine just a tiny bit less. Not a lot, but even just an ounce helps. Like taking a few food wrappers out of your car. The car is still dirty, but visually it's not as daunting.

Now I have a job to do. I have to raise my two kids and make sure they don't hate me. Do I get sad that Jack Sr. can't meet Jack the Fourth? Of course. Would the two Jacks be cute riding in a golf cart together or doing the white man's overbite on the dance floor? Would it be special for my dad to visit Jane's school when she has Grandparents' Day? Would it be fun seeing the two of them try to make each other laugh with their big cheeks?

Let's not go there.

When you are born, your dad is already a dad. He kind of became one the moment you were detected in the womb, then more officially as the doctor sees your head emerging. Or maybe when you came out, he'd already been a dad because you have an older sibling or two. You don't think anything of it. You don't go on LinkedIn to check your parents' backgrounds. *That's my dad,* you think. You assume they know what they're doing, so you have no idea what it took for the two of you to meet at this junction.

Now I know. Now I know how hard my father worked to help raise me. Jack is almost four, and Jane is almost two, and they'll be a project of mine until the day I die. I'm a doting dad. It's just my style. I'll be that dad that visits Jack at college whether he wants me to or not. I'll be intense. I'll be strict like my dad, but a worrier like my mother. It's an eye-opening process, though, to be on the other end of the life spectrum when the baby comes out and you're the one they call Daddy now.

I like to think every grandchild is a reflection of my father and a way to carry on his spirit. A way for me to be with him when the traditional way is no longer an option. A way for me to bond with him after our initial run was cut short. It's not always clearly visible what traits were passed on or when he'll show up, but some days I just know he's there without having to look.

The other day Jack farted and immediately rolled over with laughter.

Hi, Dad.

CHAPTER 19
THE GREEN CHAIR

"WHERE ARE YOU?" I asked. I could barely hear Sami on the other end of the line as Pookie and I stood in the driveway of our Nantucket house. I had her on speakerphone.

"We're on the ferry. We found some gay guys. They're sharing their wine with us." She laughed.

"Is that John?" Sarah asked in the background, sounding relaxed and a little drunk.

"Cool, Mom just arrived. What time do you get in?" I, meanwhile, was straight to the point because I was clean sober.

It was a Friday in mid-September 2020. The weather was peaking in the low sixties with bright sun and the giddiness of the holiday season on the horizon. The pandemic had been in effect for six months, and Pookie's goal of selling our family beach house on Nantucket had been in effect for seven years. Unlike COVID, our house, 'Windswept,' was no longer going strong. Pookie had made up her mind that it was finally time to sell. The house was listed in August unfortunately–or fortunately, depending on if you're me or Pookie's Realtor–then sold a month later. My older sisters and my mother and I were here for the weekend to say goodbye to a house and an island that I had been visiting for literally thirty-nine years. We also had to throw out a ton of sh*t before the movers came.

I smiled and looked at Pookie, who of course couldn't miss a conversation and had hit pause on sorting through the clutter in her car to listen. She also hadn't hit pause on just choosing one facial expression. She was shifting between four: an eye roll, a brow crunch, a smile, and strained eyes. She was off to the races. Due to her anxiety over the years Pookie had started to develop ticks in her extremities and grimaces on her face, like uncontrollable winking and eye rolling. This made it hard to tell if she was judging you or just having a muscle spasm in her face.

My sisters were set to arrive for the weekend and needed a ride once they did.

"Can you pick us up?" Sami asked. "We'd walk, but Sarah brought a suitcase like she's flying to the Bahamas. Not a duffel."

We both laughed.

"Heyyy, I didn't think it through!" Sarah said defensively.

"Sounds good. Text us as you're arriving."

An hour later my buzzed sisters piled into the car down by the wharf. They couldn't stop laughing at all the stuff they had to climb over to get in. Sami, with her knees practically up to her chest because old beach towels and bags were taking up her leg room, held up a beach bag with seashells on it from forty years ago.

"Oh! I was wondering where this was."

We all laughed; well, most of us did.

"Oh, would you stop!" Pookie yelped from the passenger seat.

"Okay, we ready? Mom, do you have three random coats in case it rains, snows, or sleets?"

Pookie paused, confused, then looked down. She had taken much of the crap from the back seat and placed it on her lap, at her sides, and over her feet to make room for my sisters. The top layer was three coats.

She shot me an eyebrow raise. "Thin ice!" she warned.

I found myself smiling as I pulled the car out of the parking space and steered away from a drunk cougar who was cluelessly about to walk right into my right headlight. This was rare, the four of us here for an entire weekend with no one else—Natalie couldn't take the time off and was more than fine being home alone. But the big factor was no kids and no spouses. The last time this had happened was probably twenty years ago. Sure, in a way this weekend was a funeral for us, losing access to our favorite place on Earth and a house that was the bridge that had brought us all together for many summers in a row. We were in mourning, but Colberts make mourning fun.

Our digs for the weekend were not exactly dumpy. Friends of Sami's were letting us stay in their beautiful four-bedroom 'guesthouse' that was right in town. It was within walking distance of restaurants, so we didn't have to worry about getting groceries. To stay in a 'Mike and Deb' house is not like staying anywhere else. It was like a Nancy Meyers movie. No inch of space was unused or neglected. Varnished carved furniture, buttery leather armchairs, even the walls were covered in linen. Deb's style was like old-world English meets curated props. There were twenty vintage tennis racquets as decoration down in the finished basement; fifteen antique model cars on a shelf in the kids' play space.

"Isn't this amazing?" Sami said as she headed up the stairs. "I think there's two bedrooms up here and then two downstairs. I figure I'll take the master since I got us this house."

No one disputed it.

"So four total, right?" I asked.

Thirty seconds in and we were already focused on the sleeping arrangements. Sarah and I followed Sami while Pookie tested out the bathroom. The second floor had natural light and an opulent master suite as well as a bedroom and en suite bath just down the hall. Sami threw herself on the master bed and immediately assumed the starfish position. She looked like she could be asleep in seconds if we let her.

"Holy–!" Sarah yelled from the master bath.

"You can use it whenever you want, Sarah," Sami offered, like we were her assistants for the weekend.

"Is anyone else famished?" Pookie asked as she entered the room.

"Yes," Sarah said.

"We have a six forty-five at Nantucket Tap Room," Sami pointed out. Which was an hour away.

Pookie made a face like that might as well be midnight.

Sami saw it. "I'm sure we could go earlier if we want."

"That would be good. Some of us haven't eaten in a while."

My sisters and I did a group eye roll.

Two hours later we were fat, drunk, and happy as we walked home from dinner. Staying in town was priceless, something we weren't used to. We were used to a fifteen-minute drive home if we ever went out, so being able to get home on foot and walk off our gluttonous meal was a treat. Some of us had enjoyed a little too much food, it seemed. As we crossed the street in front of Murray's Toggery Shop, we heard a loud horn. I stopped and turned around as Sami passed me. Sarah was in the middle of the vacant street, slightly bent over, dying laughing.

"Was that you?!" I yelled.

Sarah nodded. "My gas is so bad."

Her butt struck again, this time like the quack of a duck. I nearly peed my pants I was laughing so hard. Pookie was half a block behind us, still trying to catch up.

"Oh, awful! Sarah, that was you?" she asked. "Did you bring prunes?"

"Yeah, I keep them loose in my purse," Sarah replied as she squeaked out another tribute to our dinner. Sarah has always had lethal gas. Her husband sometimes gets mad because it can clear a room. A room he was comfortable and wanted to stay in.

We walked up the side street headed home, giggling like hyenas. Sami now joined in with zero volume awareness.

"MAN, THIS ISLAND IS JUST SO AMAZING!" She was full-on yelling and, always, turning into a podcast for positivity. "Mom, isn't it just so incredible that you are here with all your adult kids? Besides Natalie, I mean?"

Pookie approached the small hill that we just climbed, which to her might as well have been Everest. She was losing her breath quickly. Did we help? Nah. We were too busy being drunk in the dimly lit, empty streets of this old, quaint island.

"OH GOD, SARAH AND I ARE SHARING A BATH-ROOM!" I yelled. I blame my volume on the old-fashioned and two good glasses of red wine I'd had. Plus, we were alone, with not a soul in sight, hence why I found myself following Sarah's lead.

Sami suddenly turned around. "EW, DID YOU JUST FART?!"

I couldn't stop laughing. What is it about farting in public that feels wrong yet so right? Is it technically illegal? Sure feels like it. The echo off the cobblestones was fantastic. And who was going to hear us?

Two innocent guests at a nearby B&B, that's who. I didn't know it was even open until we passed by and all were blatantly staring, admiring its cozy little front patio, as a married couple sat on Adirondack chairs, sharing a bottle of wine, and, unfortunately, a whiff of Sarah's gas.

Realizing our entire journey to this point was not private, I immediately froze up and naturally flashed a nervous smile. The couple stayed serious. We stumbled on, Sarah clutching her stomach, Sami already a mile ahead, and Pookie easily four miles behind. She should've just slept at the restaurant, and we could've picked her up in the morning with the car, thrown her on the roof, and tied her down like a Christmas tree.

The next morning it was a sunny, beautiful day as we got to Windswept in Tom Nevers. We all wolfed down our greasy egg sandwiches from Downyflake in the kitchen and got to work. One of our contractors' workers, Fito, was coming around noon with a huge truck to take whatever we wanted to get rid of to the dump for free. In exchange we were giving him a ton of furniture.

It was a great deal for us, and we had our work cut out for us as the clock on the oven read 9:20 a.m. The entire kitchen had to be either packed or brought to the garage for trash. There were forty years of coffee mugs; wine glasses; five different sets of plates; old, rusty steak knives; there was even a bottle of blue curaçao from when I started to get into my bartending phase in high school twenty-five years ago.

I put on yacht rock on my phone, placed it into a bowl to act as a speaker, and we got to work packing and reminiscing.

My sisters moved at a healthy pace.

Pookie on the other hand...

"Mom, you can't take everything with you."

She was like a street cleaner doing laps and swooping up the crap no one else wanted and putting it in her boxes.

"Do you need three oil lanterns?"

"Johnny O. said he wanted one."

Her boyfriend was not helping our case.

"Fifteen plastic margarita glasses? You don't drink."

"Well..."

I had to start trailing behind her and supervising because at this rate she'd take the whole house with her. Sami was in blaze mode as she hauled box after box of crap to the garage. Sarah was sorting through what to add to her 'pile.' Each family member had started to make piles of what they wanted so that when the movers came, they would know how to load the truck.

It was around noon when Sami came in from the garage, stressed. "Fito is here with the truck and his entire family. We need to beat feet!"

"Shit," Sarah said as she looked over to the kitchen and saw most of the cupboards' contents still lay on the countertop. Like a timer had just been set, we all sprinted to the kitchen and began tossing stuff into boxes to run out to the garage. "Does anyone have any fruit?" she added because that really was necessary at his moment.

Sami was already back. "Anything you don't want, like furniture, paintings... bring it out there to see if his family wants it or they'll trash it."

"Sarah wants fruit," I added.

"Literally fruit, nothing specific?" Sami added.

Sarah was *frangry*–fruit hangry. "I'm just dying for a piece of fruit. Like a peach or banana. We don't have anything in the fridge?"

"Not unless you brought it!" Pookie barked as she walked by holding four different woven baskets that we had put in the trash pile not an hour ago.

"No one else is craving fruit? I feel like we've had none all weekend."

"We really need to hurry. Fito is already here for the first load. Maybe he'll have fruit," Sami said as she grabbed a box and headed toward the garage.

I power-walked over to the living room to inspect my pile and to see if there was anything worth adding to the outside trash pile.

"Do I want this broken lamp?" Sarah narrated as she stood over her pile twenty feet away. She was inspecting an old kitschy lamp that had a little painted fisherman as its base. It was garbage but nostalgic. "Jonathan could probably fix it. I could paint it. Maybe it would go into Madelyn's room."

"Do you want another project?" I asked. I felt like I made a good point, but I watched as she bit her lip and put it back in her pile. I don't know why I bothered, but I didn't have time to waste. On my pile, there were four armchairs, all different types, that I was contemplating pitching. In times like these I like to dig deep... into my pocket and pull out my phone to text Jill, the interior designer. I typed, followed by a pic, *Do these go with our dining room table?*

Nope, she typed back instantly and decisively. Definitely not a Colbert.

I grabbed one and brought it outside. Fito's family was going through the stuff to see what was decent and what was trash. We introduced ourselves. I made a corny joke. They laughed. I liked them. I put a green, wooden chair down and headed back inside to find Sarah with her hands on her hips, scoping out my pile. She noticed the one chair of the four was now gone. She, like Pookie, is a hoarder.

"You're getting rid of the armchairs?" she asked.

That's when the doubt started to set in. "Yeah, they're not all the same set."

"Might be good to have, though. It's annoying buying that kind of stuff once you have a house."

Now I was biting my lip. Twenty-four hours with my sister and suddenly I couldn't be confident in my decisions. "I already put it outside, though, in the 'pile.'"

Sarah was amused. "Just go grab it."

"Can I do that?"

"Sure."

I walked outside to the front yard and without missing a beat did a U-turn and came back inside.

"Fito's wife is sitting in it! She looks very comfortable!"

Sarah and I were now laughing as we went back out to

233

snoop on Fito's wife and the green chair. Head of CIA recruitment, if you're reading this, never let us in. While we think we're slick, we're most definitely not. Sarah went out through the garage and pretended to check out a box of books while I went out the front door to flank her from the left. We needed Mrs. Fito to get up so we could snag the chair back. But how would we get her up? Our tactic so far seemed to be a combination of frantic walking around the exterior of the house while biting our nails.

I knew what I had to do. I had to man up and text Jill. *Are we sure we don't want that chair?* I texted. *It's growing on me.* But also I couldn't get it back so I needed reassurance that, yes, it was worth donating. Sarah made a good point. For twenty years I had always said no to furniture because roaming from city to city I never had the space for it. Jill and I were in the market to find a house in the 'burbs, and the image of moving into one with no furniture in any rooms or accruing insane credit debt to fill them was scaring me. It was me versus the nice woman sitting in it. I've faced greater obstacles, trust me, but I waited to get Jill's response and approval. I took another look at the target. She was settling in all right in that antique chair. As she should. I think technically the moment her ass started to generate heat on it, it was officially hers. Plus, who could blame her? She's been watching four loon-bag white people run back and forth to empty their beach house into piles to be taken to the dump, from books to coffee mugs to random chairs. This one was in the donation pile, so of course it was fair game. But still, she really had some nerve.

I looked down at my phone, then back up. I didn't know what else to do or where else to go. Pookie was a goner as far as taking duplicates of things, and Sarah's demand for fruit was dead on arrival. I was ready to go back inside and be helpful when I heard the wheels of a bike roll across the seashell drive. Sarah was wheeling an old bike into the trash, and as I watched her, she suddenly got excited. She motioned towards Mrs. Fito and whisper-screamed, "She's gone!" I peered my head around the porch column to see that she was right. The chair was vacant!

I sprinted off the porch, stubbed my toe in the process, and nearly tripped and died. I was *ride or die* for this freakin' armchair! Pain is weakness leaving the body, and I'm the kind of guy that will take free furniture but pay sixteen dollars for a cocktail. I didn't have time to acknowledge my toe. I was wearing sneakers, but it definitely felt like I nailed the big one. Damn these flat clown feet. As I walked briskly towards the empty chair, the pain started to wear off. I spotted Fito and his wife and son deep in the garage. I then did what any mature adult in my situation would do: I coughed like I was covering up for the loud sound I was making, even though it was quite silent, and tried not to laugh as I picked the chair up by the arms and headed back in through the front door, away from the garage (i.e., the witnesses), and put the green armchair back in my pile of crap. Piece of shit, party of one, here at your service. I felt relieved. I felt excited. I also felt a vibration and pulled my phone out. Jill had replied.

No, screw it.

GOD DAMN IT. Drenched in sweat I put the armchair back in the exact spot I had just stolen it from.

As I watched us all slowly unload that house and all its memories, it hit me that this was the end of an era. I got thirty-nine years out of Windswept. Almost forty years of nostalgia tied to the island, the house, and so many of the items inside of it. Like the old round table in the kitchen that I'd do arts and crafts on when I was little. Or the set of salt-water fishing rods in the garage that my dad and I used to surf cast with after dinner. But there was a silver lining. Seeing a lot of these items go to a good family like Fito's was heartwarming. I couldn't help but smile at the idea of them making new memories with them as did my family over the years. It was like seeing everything get a second life with another family was giving me, dare I say it—joy?

Plus, it made my shipping bill to Pennsylvania cheaper.

CHAPTER 20
HUG THE ONES YOU'RE WITH

A FEW MONTHS before that fateful New Year's Eve in 2001, when my father went to the ER in his black tux en route to a party, he and I shared a nice little morning together at the breakfast table. A beautiful, antique Irish farm table to be specific. It was about nine a.m. on a cool yet sunny fall day in New England. Some rays of sunshine were piercing through the foliage, magnified through the glass windows around us before they hit our faces.

It was fucking lovely.

He was engrossed in the latest issue of the the *Boston Globe*. I, a Best Buy circular. He was learning about current affairs. I was learning about current TV sales. Yes, my father was much more intellectual than I. Thought that was a given from the get-go.

I believe I was home from college for Columbus Day weekend to see my family whom I love so much. I also had mountains of laundry to do. The sweet smell of Natty Light and Abercrombie Woods cologne wasn't going to wash itself out.

Regardless of why I was home, I do remember that a shiny, new Sony receiver going on sale in the circular had caught my eye when a familiar voice broke my tech-nerd focus.

"You have a big birthday coming up this spring. The big two-one," he casually pointed out, excited as he lowered the paper, giving me a clear view of my upbeat dad. He was in his usual corporate costume: a nice Brooks Brothers suit and a tie, most likely with a nice pattern on it. Like knights in armor.

"Sure do," I said with a slightly evil grin. I couldn't wait to be able to drink with my siblings in a bar. Well, at least legally.

My dad chuckled at my reply. Before he returned to his paper, he concluded with, "We'll have to go out and get beers to celebrate."

COUNT ME IN!

Why wouldn't I? My dad was always a man of his word, and I like to think I am too. It's why when people are *all talk* and *no do* it's a major pet peeve. So here we were. An idea was floated across the table, and I had confirmed it to make it so. This was just a beer or two to celebrate me becoming of legal drinking age. Nothing fancy, nothing ambitious. Nothing in my mind that day made me think it wasn't possible.

Nothing could have been further from the truth.

As you may recall, on March 22, 2002, my father took his last breaths in the ICU at Brigham & Women's Hospital in Boston, five months after our nice breakfast chat and, even worse, two weeks shy of my twenty-first birthday. *The* birthday he and I were probably the most looking forward to celebrating together. Others were just for me, but this was the one that benefited us both.

Trust me, I got plenty of beers the night of my birthday. In fact I drank so much thanks to a handful of fraternity brothers taking me out in Keene that I ralphed over the railing of my front porch all night. It's not like I haven't been fortunate enough to enjoy drinks with fantastic company in exotic places. There's been Champagne tasting in France, wine pairings at Michelin- starred restaurants in New York, and even ice cold beers after surfing in Bali.

But no matter how special the drink, location, or people I'm able to share it with, I still long for that one beer with my father like he promised, let alone any beer with my father. When I want to celebrate something, or life has me down and I really just need a dad's input, my dad's input, I'd really kill to have him join me for a drink.

While this is sad as hell, I'm not here to depress you. In fact I want to do the opposite. I want to inspire and scare you into appreciating the people that are still breathing in your life. Trust me, no one knows how annoying family can be more than I do. I have three sisters. That's right, three women in my family in addition to my mother and my wife. But when they're gone, there's no going back. How else am I going to learn the importance of getting my colon checked five years before every doctor suggests it?

Now that I'm in my forties some of my friends have also lost their dads, and others have lost their mothers. I always wonder what life would be like had we lost Pookie instead of Pake. It sounds bleak, but it's a natural question to ask. Not out loud in front of my mother, of course, but what would that do to the family dynamic? Or the emotional intelligence of a child, let alone a boy on the brink of becoming a man?

When you lose someone, years later you fantasize about what life would be like if they were still around. Would my father take me out to dinner if he was in town on business? Would he have made my wedding weekend that much more fun since I learned how to host from him? Would he have bought my wife and me our first home? Probably not, but it's fun to dream!

The grass isn't always greener. On days I miss my father, I have a friend who complains about his who is still living. He lost his mom a few years after I lost my dad, so we have opposite problems. Thanks to him I've learned there's a comforting nature that moms are great at. He doesn't get that anymore. He does get a sounding board of wisdom that only dads can offer and which is of great value to sons.

How do I feel about people who still have both parents?

Hate them. Obviously.

While I often joke about being 'damaged goods' ever since my father passed away, I've learned it's actually far from the truth. Okay, 'far' is an extreme word. I definitely have had some shaky screws loose ever since 2002, but not all side effects are negative. There are plenty of product benefits as well. When you lose something quite valuable in your life, it's like losing a key body part. You're forced to build up certain skills to compensate for the loss.

Like how blind people can smell a belch four miles away. That sounds more like a curse than a gift. But you get the idea.

When you lose a loved one, you develop a sixth sense. You can't see through walls, but you can see a little bit above the clouds compared to everyone else. You are able to make smarter choices because you know you can't take life for granted. You're not always more mature, just less wasteful. I still complain about trivial things like a bad parking space or a coffee shop only having half and half, but I also know to say yes to social plans when someone is in town even though I'm exhausted. What if they're never in town again?

Your level of compassion for others skyrockets. When I was nineteen, I was selfish and clueless to the pain of others. Now I have a goddamn black belt in that shit. I'll go to the funeral of a coworker's parent even though I think the guy kinda sucks at his job. I go because I know how huge it was for me when my entire fraternity showed up in the receiving line at my father's wake. They drove two hours from New Hampshire. All you need are familiar people by your side. Plus, when one leans in and giggles during the receiving line while making a dirty joke, it's a priceless distraction from the tragedy at hand.

You learn to be the strength for others because you're much more healed than they are at their time of grief. This is what I did when my best friend, Greg, told me that his father had passed away. I had known Mr. Rubin since I was in third grade. He had an amazingly corny sense of humor and had nick-named me "JJ" years ago because of our predictable phone banter. Every time I'd call Greg's house to see if he was around to chat or hang out, it was the same exact convo.

"Hi, is Greg there?" I'd ask from my end of the landline.

"No he's not," Steve (Mr. Rubin) would say. "May I tell him who called?"

"It's just John."

"JJ!" he'd exclaim excitedly.

"Huh?" I said the first time he said that.

"JJ. Just John," he'd explain.

"Oh, now I get it," I'd say. That conversation happened every single time thereafter. Minus the explanation.

I was new at a job in LA when Greg called and broke the news. His father, who had had ALS for a few years and lately had had round-the-clock care because of the severity of it, had sadly passed away peacefully at home. Fortunately, he would no longer be in pain. In his last year or so, he had lost the ability to talk, having to write things out on pads of paper. For such a smart, business-savvy, funny man—whose every utterance was either a wise insight or genius pun—to take away his voice was not an inconvenience; it was a deal breaker. I give him credit for fighting for so long. I would've given up the day doctors told me, "We wanna do some tests."

I stayed strong for Greg while I was on the phone with him as I stood on the rooftop of the ad agency I worked for, overlooking Culver City and a beautiful skyline beyond. Greg and I chatted for a bit, even just catching up on all things random, like my new apartment and making fun of his mom's book club. After a bit I told him I was going to look into flights for the funeral. He said thank you and hung up. It was a nice chat, even if it was a death that made us catch up.

I smiled to myself, looked back up at the bright pink sky over my head, and then broke out into tears. It wasn't a beautiful cry. If you'd seen it, you would have been like, "Oh... oh god. That man is not right."

I don't know if I was more upset that someone I had known and admired for so long had passed or because I, sadly more so than anyone else, knew what Greg's future would be like emotionally, having just spent the past eleven years fatherless myself. I knew about those damn five to twelve stages of grief (depending on who you ask) and all the garbage it brings with it. Although he will get those baller free meals for a bit, such as "Lisa's" heavenly casserole. Lord knows I did!

Two days later I was on a red-eye to Boston. It was my job to be there for my buddy now that he was part of the worst club of all time. It also feels really good helping others. And... I may or may not have missed the East Coast and was looking for an excuse to visit.

The trip was quick. The trip was exhausting. The trip was extremely well worth it. I saw Pookie. I saw Greg's mom, Mrs. Rubin, also known as 'Bubbles.' I saw his siblings Matt and Jess. We all even did a shot together from a double magnum bottle of Chivas that Mr. Rubin had been saving for, and I quote, "when he dies." Everyone was in good spirits. It's how my dad's funerary events were, and I highly recommend it.

What I've learned since my father's death, and what people like my bestie Greg have learned since his father passed, is death can come quick and out of the blue. We don't know how much longer we and the ones we're with will be around. It's terrifying yet beautiful at the same time because it keeps us on our toes.

You'll find, though, that even if you may not treasure them now, you will when they're gone. And by then it's too late. You'll find yourself in Regret City with nothing but a sweet dosage of depression, wishing you had done more with them. Wishing you had turned so many moments into fun ones instead of sweating the small stuff.

Spend time with friends and family who are still breathing,

even if they suck sometimes. Turn it around and make them laugh. You won't regret it, and then if they do get cancer and pass away years from now, you'll feel good knowing you didn't waste a second when they were healthy. You'll also think of me and how amazingly helpful I was. See? I'm a really good friend!

Here's my last unsolicited rant of wisdom. Listen up...

If you can call your dad, do it. Tell him something trivial or impressive you did today. Because I can't. I had big news today (yes, literally today as I write this) and all I wanna do is pick up the phone and brag to my dad about it. My news happens to be business-related, and he was a samurai with that stuff. Plus, he was my dad.

Now stop sitting on your 'fanny,' as Pookie would say and put this book down and go spend time with a loved one. Especially if they're old and sick. Don't make plans to have a drink. Just have that drink. Because, take it from me, there are no second chances.

Unless you have a time machine. In that case, let's talk.

ABOUT THE AUTHOR

JOHN COLBERT learned how to be an "okay" writer by working in advertising as a copywriter on brands like Taco Bell and 7 Eleven. When he's not writing books or commercials he's spending quality time with his roommates who also happen to be his wife and kids. They reside with their dog Koji in the suburbs of Pennsylvania where everyone is obsessed with the Eagles. Go birds?

www.ingramcontent.com/pod-product-compliance
Lightning Source LLC
Chambersburg PA
CBHW021222130626
46554CB00004B/1324